"Love fast, live slow is not a catchy phrase or clever mantra for a select sub group. It is a biblically based, practical invitation to us all to live a God honoring, simplified life; one we would do well to accept in this stress-filled life."

Cheryl Rice, Pastor's Wife & Bible Teacher at
Calvary Church, Clearwater, FL

"In a day when society tells us to go faster and look out for ourselves it seems everyone is more exasperated and on edge. Nick and Laura Mendenhall offer a refreshing challenge to love fast and live slow. Their personal stories inspire a fresh outlook on life and challenge the reader to take a step back, breath deep, and love big."

Derrick Fielder, Lead Pastor of LaFayette First
Baptist Church

"Within the pages of this book your worldview will be flipped upside down. You will laugh, cry and completely relate to Nick and Laura as they guide you through the message God has given them to share with the world."

Jenna Blair, Full-time mentor to young adults
pursuing ministry in the 10/40 window

"The time has never been more right for you to read this. This book is filled with authentic vulnerability about failures and success we can all relate with. I laughed, cried, and felt convicted as I took an introspective look within. The world needs us all read this."

Kelly Reynolds, Corporate Learning & Development,
Chick-fil-A Inc.

Love Fast Live Slow

By Nick and Laura Mendenhall

CONTENTS

FORWARD

Meetings, errands, demands, deadlines, projects, family, obligations, and more can create an enormous distraction and stress. My day is often consumed and overwhelmed with the layers of stress that each of these brings. As a child of God I deeply desire connection with Him and to be a conduit of His grace to others, but sometimes I get in my own way. Does that sound familiar?

If you are honest, you likely relate, and stories flood your mind of how all-consuming the rhythms of your life may beat to a cadence that contradicts the Spirit of God and even contradicts your heartfelt desire. In the midst of that reality enters a clear and honest book. *Love Fast Live Slow* is written with sincerity and relatability to call us into a clear and focused pursuit of God and expression of His love to the world around us.

As a pastor, I spend countless hours coaching individuals as they navigate the stresses of life. My heart is often heavy as I carry their burdens with them. The thoughts and challenges that Nick and Laura expose in this book are truly inspirational and relevant.

I have known Nick and Laura for many years and can testify to the genuineness of their convictions and life. Laura was a part of my student ministry through middle and high school. She was an integral part of our student leadership and actively pursued the Lord. Needless to say, I was guarded when Nick started pursuing her. Like most youth pastors, we consider students in our ministry like our own, so I was careful to check this guy out. I quickly began to develop a deep love for him and value his commitment to lead worship, conduct ministry, and care deeply for Laura. It was my honor, in fact, to officiate their wedding.

I will never forget that day as he and I both were watching Georgia Bulldogs intently right up to the moment we had to rush out for the ceremony. In fact, if we were a minute late Laura, we are sorry...sort of.

Nick and Laura believe and profess what they write in this book. As you will read, "If you chase the gift instead of the Giver, you will never be satisfied." It is part of the core of their being that you grasp a connection to the Creator and rest in His deep love for you. That soul-level satisfaction will enable you to inhale the peace that comes when we slow down and rest in His presence, and exhale His never-ending love in your relationships.

You and I will likely continue to have meetings, stressors, and urgency into our day, but the impact of this book will challenge your heart, encourage your soul, and prayerfully guide you to make some slight alterations to the rhythm of your life that can have an everlasting impact.

In Christ,

Dr. Ricky Smith
@rickylamarsmith
Lead Pastor, Calvary Baptist Church, Columbus, GA

Dedicated to anyone we've ever stepped over, tuned out or overlooked in the pursuit of selfish ambition. Jesus wouldn't do that and, by God's grace, He's given us this message to share.

INTRODUCTION

We'll cut to the chase. The book you have opened is full of stories, Scripture, and real-life application to help generate a calm in your storm. Oftentimes we come to God begging for clarity on our next best step, and He unarms us with the reminder, "I'll let you know what you need to know when you need to know it. In the meantime, do what I've already told you." And what we know we should be doing, rain or shine, clear or foggy, is to live like Jesus did. That is why *Love Fast Live Slow* exists.

I Was Off Track - Laura

I I had just had a meltdown—the kind with uncontrollable, hysterical tears and short, sharp breaths to remind my lungs to keep me alive. Definitely an ugly cry. Nick had just arrived home from a long work day. I had missed my favorite spin class by seven minutes, but my hysteria wasn't due to that absence. The frustration over the absence was the scapegoat. Although the exercise endorphins might have been helpful, Nick knew something greater was coming undone inside of me as I sat on our living room floor with tears streaming down my cheeks.

As I attempted to unsuccessfully hide the puddle forming on my shirt sleeves, he cracked the Hoover Dam of emotions and asked, "Are you okay?"

Then it happened.

I lost it.

How dare he not know every emotion I felt and every sacrifice I had been making. "Am I okay? Am I okay, Nick?" I snapped. The slow path of tears turned into a loud, soggy monsoon no one had seen coming. I put down our newborn daughter because heaven forbid black mascara tears fall on her beautiful complexion. Our two boys slid into the arena as they peeked their heads around the corner. I rushed to our bedroom, ashamed of my lack of control.

Nick timidly slithered into the room where I was hiding. "Do you want to talk?" At that point, my face had already turned patchy red, and he was close enough to catch the weight of my shoulders falling into him. I buried my head in his chest and declared, "I'm not strong enough. I'm just not strong enough for this."

We Were All off Track - Nick

Sometimes there are moments we can never escape—moments that change everything as we know it. I was completely unaware that we were in one of these life-changing seasons. I was blind to the magnitude of Laura's distress because I had been working long hours and was focused on building a new business. Not that I was unaware of the challenges facing my family. I was acutely aware. Where I was clueless was in how Laura was dealing with these challenges compared to how I was dealing with them.

I'm a big ball of emotions most of the time. Not the crying kind but the wear-my-emotions-on-my-sleeve kind. I tend to share my feelings with anyone and everyone who will listen. It's both a blessing and a curse. A blessing because I tend not to have massive blow-ups from holding stuff in too long and a curse because I have blow-ups from letting my emotions out anytime they well up. The biggest problem with my way of handling emotions is that I have to do a lot of apologizing as part of the aftermath of my rampages. Most often there is no guess work in knowing how something makes me feel. For Laura, I have to be super intentional to look and ask for the things going on inside her head. She keeps stuff in far better than I do. It's actually been a major point of contention in our marriage. It makes for some interesting moments in our family.

When Laura said she was not strong enough, I mistakenly made some sarcastic comment, quoting Will Farrell from *Saturday Night Live*. I told her she was "coming at me like a tornado of teeth and fingernails" in my best Harry Caray voice. Not the best choice on my part. Her brokenness was necessary to make it possible for me to see the depth of her struggle—necessary because if one member of our family is misaligned, we're all off track.

Turning Point - Laura

I don't want to isolate this meltdown as the only turning point in our lives. Every quarter I have a good cry; it's good for the soul (am I right, ladies?). Why? Because parenting is hard, bills are hard, marriage is hard, work is hard, faith is hard. By March 2018, we had a 12-week old baby, two energetic boys, hospital bills filling our dining room table, and pending requests to see our newly listed home that was justifiably trashed.

I was feeling the pressure of picking up new projects at

work to earn some additional cash flow, and we'd been praying for Nick to find full-time work. And wouldn't you know, in God's "perfect timing" (sarcasm mine) Nick started a new business the week we put our house on the market. I felt like I could have been the star of *The Truman Show*. The plot thickened daily, and we could either numb out or face the mountain ahead of us.

We all have those days. Weeks. Years. Nick and I are real people. Just a real family who struggles with real problems. You too? Then you are in the right place. Keep reading. Life is full of ups and downs, some of which we can control and some we cannot. The defining moment is how you respond to life when the ground is shaky. That is why we chose to write this book. God has much to say about love, peace, forgiveness, and faith. But what about pain, anger, confusion, and weakness? How are we supposed to respond when life just sucks? We've decided that in all circumstances, the answer is to love fast and live slow.

The following chapters will walk you through a series of stories and life lessons that we've learned the hard way. Our hope is that you laugh and cry with us along the way. Pain hurts, and we all feel it as we trudge through the valley and hold on for dear life through the wild roller coasters of life. God designed us to be in a relationship with Him. Our greatest gift in return should be to accept the season we are in and trust His pace and place in it all.

We feel underqualified to write a book about living a peaceful and purposeful life. Also, it seems a bit romanticized. Skim the aisles of any bookstore or Amazon Best Seller list, and you are sure to find fancy self-help books reminding you to live your best life. Many people write about compassion and acts of philanthropy. Many people teach self-care and productivity hacks. Yet the rise of those with anxiety and depression is growing in unprecedented numbers. Antidepressant usage has increased 400 percent since 1994.[1] The global suicide mortality rate is predicted to be one death every 20 seconds by 2020.[2] Fear of the unknown impacts every inch of our daily lives, from pesticides on food to lead in our water, road rage, terrorist attacks, and school shootings.[3] Humanity is overwhelmed with feelings of distress now more than ever. The world is looking for a solution to the angst.

A trending solution to this overarching misalignment is to fill our lives with more. More stuff. More money. More exercise. More volunteering. More prestige. We look outward to satisfy our hunger for happiness. When the pendulum swings too far in our pursuit for more, it leads us to counter that busyness with a desperate evacuation: having less, doing less, spending less, conquering less. We see this trend expanding as shows like *Tidy Up* and the minimalist movement climb the charts. However, owning less or doing less is still an external solution to an internal problem.

Crumbling on the floor of my bedroom in a soggy mess was simply a byproduct of all the instability and stress I felt from carrying more weight than usual (metaphorically and literally). However, busyness can be unavoidable in certain seasons of our lives, especially the career-building and child-rearing years. If you've ever reached the end of your rope, red flags popped up along the way. A surefire way to create destruction in your life is to ignore those red flags. Our culture has grown accustomed to barreling on through caution lights because slowing down seems too risky. We are often set up to believe this life is a race: the one who gets the highest score the fastest wins. However, slowing down is better. Jesus waited, rested, recharged, and took one step at a time. I don't know about you, but I'm going to follow His lead.

Love Fast Live Slow Filter

Whether yesterday, today, or tomorrow, you will come face-to-face with feelings of unrest. You will hit bumps in the road. You will be tested and challenged to look in the mirror and ask yourself hard questions. What will your attitude be when you've hit rock bottom? Will you still live surrendered at your highest peak? Our natural instinct is to combat those feelings with whatever strength we can muster in order to avoid becoming a "soggy mess." Whether it's related to work, marriage, parenting, finances, or health (the list could go on), we challenge you to apply these Love Fast Live Slow principles. To live like Jesus, we must train our hearts and minds to slow down and let love become a natural reflex.

Within the pages of this book, we lay out what the Love Fast Live Slow mindset entails. Our life applications are rooted in what the Bible says about living a full and abundant life. No matter what the world says, we can choose to find rest and peace in Him. And Him alone. Rest and peace are not the result of our own might or power because we aren't as strong as we think. When you feel weak, it's His chance to show off. When you feel under pressure, brag on God. When you feel inadequate, ask God to remind you Who He is (not seeking validation in who you are). It's not about us. We aren't the heroes. We are along for the ride, but every choice we make can have a greater impact on the world when we choose to love fast and live slow.

To live like Jesus, we must train our hearts and minds to slow down and let love become a natural reflex.

CHAPTER ONE

First Comes Love

"There is a way that appears to be right,
but in the end it leads to death" (Proverbs 14:12).

Taking our eyes off ourselves and placing them on Jesus is the only way to live our best life. To know Him, to love Him, and to make Him known are the ultimate ways to ground yourself in love. All other pursuits pale in comparison. God's way of doing things is unconventional (like washing dirty feet, which we will talk about later in the chapter). To be rooted in love, let's first pull some weeds that suffocate our progress.

As a society, we place more value on what we have achieved as individuals than on our value in a family and community. I (Nick) am sure this thought comes as no surprise. We've tried to justify selfish tendencies, and it's driving us further away from the selfless love Jesus teaches. The media glorifies self-gratification, and it's become standard to strive (whatever the cost) for success, live with excess, and expect everything at the speed of express. This way of living is toxic.

Success, Excess and Express - Nick

First, the need to feel successful is one of, if not the most driving force in our society. We long to feel successful and approved by our family, peers, and colleagues. We've let that drive for success become so great that it is actually one of the root causes for all of our anxiety, stress, and hurt. Crazy, right? Think about it like this: the thing you want the most is not to feel stress or anxiety…so you tell yourself success will help…so you work harder and harder and become a workaholic…which compounds the stress and anxiety. It doesn't make sense.

Secondly, excess is an area we easily overlook. It looks different for every individual. If I start comparing the stuff in my life to that of a friend I met while serving on a missions trip to Jamaica, I sure do appreciate what I have and see how blessed I am. But when I compare the stuff I have to that of some local friends who have far more money than I do, I can start to beat myself up, becoming envious or jealous. Comparison can cause my mind to wander to toxic places.

The drive for excess in our lives leads us to a place of ungratefulness. I am convinced that ungratefulness is one of the darkest places we can end up. Comparison will do that. The reason it's called excess is that it is unnecessary. We don't need it. It's not useless per se, but we certainly can live without it. I'm not saying having stuff is bad. I am saying that looking for constant excess will lead to a low place, and it begins with comparison.

Thirdly, we want everything yesterday. If there isn't an express option, it's ancient. The speed at which we expect life to happen for us is breakneck. We've created "express lanes" for driving on the expressway because our regular expressway is not fast enough. We put express lanes in grocery stores for those who have fewer items. We choose express delivery, express checkout, fast food mobile ordering for express pickup, and American Express cards to pay for our other express choices.

Our need for speed in life is rivaled only by our need for approval and more stuff. What if all this speed leads to destruction because it's just not the way God intended us to live? What if because we are designed with eternity in our hearts, we were meant to slow down, buy less, and give more? What if we were meant to embrace the time we have on this earth because we are here for more than personal satisfaction and contentment? What if we used our time to step back, slow down, and love others? When we choose to set our eyes on Him, we are choosing the unconventional path. We are choosing to love first.

Putting Others First - Laura

A great example of putting love first occurred when Jesus washed His disciples' stinky feet. I have to say, this story humbles me every time I read it. If we believe everything Jesus says, then we must do what He has done. Does this mean we are to physically wash the feet of those around us when we are facing adversity? Maybe. Maybe not. When it comes to selflessness and setting our eyes on what really matters, feet washing is high on the list of examples to follow.

In Biblical times people wore sandals everywhere, so their feet weren't just a little dusty. Oh, no, far worse. People roamed the land where oxen, horses, donkeys, and camels lived and walked. Also, as shepherds moved from town to town, their sheep left behind quite the stink on the ground. Yes, I'm talking about poop. I bet you didn't think you'd read about poop today (or maybe you are in the potty training days and poop is your life). I digress. In Jesus's day, the roads were a mixture of dirt, rocks, and aromatic leftovers from the animals. Feet weren't merely dusty; they were disgusting. The job of washing someone's feet before they entered into a house as a sign of the family's hospitality was relegated to servants.

Hospitality was a highly regarded virtue in Biblical times, especially for religious leaders. It was also important in the Jewish community. Woven into the teachings of that day and the Scriptures, hospitality was both commanded and commended. Then and now, one of the first books covered in early Jewish education is the Jewish Law as described in Leviticus.

"When a foreigner resides among you in your land, do not mistreat them. The foreigner residing among you must be treated as your native-born. Love them as yourself, for you were foreigners in Egypt. I am the LORD your God" (Leviticus 19:33-34).

To wash a guest's feet was not only good hygiene (because who wants guests to track stink all over their house), but it was also equivalent to our modern-day welcome message of *mi casa, es su casa*. My house is your house. And the wealthier you were, the more you'd demonstrate your prestige by relegating this act of servitude to the lowest on the totem pole. While the servants scurried to bring water basins and towels, you and your guests could cut right to the chase and talk business. No time to waste. No time to acknowledge this humble act. No time to return the favor.

On the days leading up to Jesus's death, a great tension existed between the religious leaders and Jesus and His crew. Pharisees prided themselves on observing tradition and abiding by the written law. On more than one occasion, they tried to trick Jesus by twisting Scriptures and asking conflicting questions to trap Him at His own game. Since all Scripture is inspired by God and Jesus is God, He had zero chance of contradicting Himself. He combatted their accusations with mind-blowing analogies and stories of grace.

His teachings were radical, unlike anything they had heard before. Just as in the game of telephone, what had originally been God-inspired teachings were now being misquoted, misinterpreted, redefined, and universally accepted as truth. The haughty religious leaders of that time were so caught up in sin that the rituals they practiced had become filthy, shallow acts of worship, including the act of washing feet. What God had established as an act of love and humility, sin had manipulated into a performance of hierarchy.

Jesus, being the trailblazer He is, continued to break down any barriers and plow through any arrogance in His path. Days before His death, He chose, of all things, to redefine the ritual of foot washing. And boy, am I grateful. Jesus already knew what was to come later that night. The betrayal. The suffering. The heartache. Yet the King of Kings and the Lord of Lords in humility performed a selfless act of service by washing His disciples' feet, including the feet of Judas, the one who would betray Him.

"[Jesus] got up from the meal, took off his outer clothing, and wrapped a towel around his waist. 5After that, he poured water into a basin and began to wash his disciples' feet, drying them with the towel that was wrapped around him. 6He came to Simon Peter, who said to him, 'Lord, are you going to wash my feet?'" (John 13:4-6).

I feel ya, Peter. Talk about a plot twist. Jesus lowering Himself to the equivalent of a servant? What did Jesus on His hands and knees washing their feet before the Passover mean? Perhaps in that moment, the disciples were kicking themselves for not washing His feet first. Maybe the disciples, just for a second, enjoyed the luxury, especially since they had just argued over who would sit beside Jesus in heaven (Mark 10:37). Did they enjoy the flattery? Or were they ashamed of not showing Him that hospitality? How would you have felt?

"Jesus replied, 'You do not realize now what I am doing, but later you will understand.'
8'No,' said Peter, 'you shall never wash my feet.'
Jesus answered, 'Unless I wash you, you have no part with me.'
9'Then, Lord,' Simon Peter replied, 'not just my feet but my hands and my head as well!'
10Jesus answered, 'Those who have had a bath need only to wash their feet; their whole body is clean. And you are clean, though not every one of you.' 11For He knew who was going to betray Him, and that was why He said not everyone was clean" (John 13:7-11).

Pause. Did you catch that? "You do not realize now what I am doing, but later you will understand." Jesus was already in mental distress about facing His crucifixion later that week. He knew the hardships that would swallow tomorrow. He has that power. He is awesome like that. But for us laymen who don't know the future, He is demonstrating how we should respond to distress, unforeseen hardships, and coming pain that may swallow tomorrow. He washes feet. He humbles himself. That is how we should respond.

> "When He had finished washing their feet, He put on His clothes and returned to His place. 'Do you understand what I have done for you?' He asked them. 13'You call me "Teacher" and "Lord," and rightly so, for that is what I am. 14Now that I, your Lord and Teacher, have washed your feet, you also should wash one another's feet" (John 13:12-14).

Jesus didn't care what was socially acceptable. Jesus wasn't afraid to get a little dirty. He didn't compromise truth to avoid conflict. He felt fear and didn't seek pity from His followers to comfort the pain. He chose to spend His last free hours in fellowship. Jesus had compassion and chose to live in that moment. He wasn't looking at His phone for the latest text, "like," or affirmation. He was washing feet to set an example for us all—an example that was beyond ritual hospitality and toxic arrogance. It was to show us what selfless love looks like in action.

To love fast and live slow is to follow Jesus's example and always love first (even when you are in a storm).

CHAPTER TWO

Then Comes Marriage

*"In your relationships with one another, have the same
mindset as Christ Jesus" (Philippians 2:5).*

OncOnce upon a time, a little country girl and a guitar-playing boy fell in love. They got married and had
some kids. The End. Or at least that's what we thought we
signed up for. Thankfully our life has been much more climactic than some standard fairy tale. If God had answered
every safe prayer request, I (Laura) think our marriage would
be far less dangerous to the Enemy. Much like any marriage,
especially one that publicly proclaims to be unified in Christ,
we've been stretched and tested. Sometimes it feels like we've
been hit by a train. The soul and doo-wop girl group of the
60s (The Shirelles) was right, "Mama said there'll be days like
this, my mama said (Mama said, mama said)."

Subconsciously, we brought habits (good and bad) into
our marriage that we had observed in our parents. Hot topics
like budget, work hours, and fighting fair were ticking time
bombs. My point here is that whatever you assume about

marriage, it takes a lot of growth to achieve bliss. When we think of marriage, we think of love. When we think of love, we think of romance. Since God is love, can God also be a romantic? According to Webster, a *romantic* is "one who is conducive to or characterized by the expression of love." And since God is love, God is romantic. This is getting fun.

God is the One Who can ultimately teach us how to love and how to receive love. How can we demonstrate love? We find the answer in the book of John, "Greater love has no one than this: to lay down one's life for one's friends" (John 15:13). Again in Ephesians, "Follow God's example... *and walk in the way of love, just as Christ loved us and gave himself up* for us as a fragrant offering and sacrifice to God" (Ephesians 5:1-2, emphasis added). The pattern we see here reveals that love equals giving yourself to another. This could not be more true in marriage.

To The Husbands - Nick

I am broken. There's no question about it. When we try to be the men we are called to be in our homes, we will fall, fail, and screw it all up apart from God's grace and His leading. I've been there. I seem to find myself there fairly often, actually. I'm not one to perpetuate a myth, created by making things appear to be something they are not. We are broken. Even in the wholeness of God's grace, we live in the broken state of humanity this side of heaven, and because of that, we will be broken to an extent until we depart this fallen world.

Now that the depressing part is out of the way, let's look at the rest of the picture and see how good God is and what He wants for us as husbands.

"Husbands, love your wives, just as Christ loved the church and gave himself up for her" (Ephesians 5:25).

At first glance, this verse might be easy to run past. We might think, "Oh, I understand that..." and move on to the next verse. But marriage takes work, and to love our spouse like Christ loved the church is immensely difficult. Loving strangers can seem easier sometimes than loving those in our own home, at least when it comes to giving of ourselves.

I'm often the first person to help someone in need, be it fixing a friend's house or volunteering for an event at church. That is in addition to leading a student ministry on Wednesday nights and Sunday mornings. That is also in addition to working full-time trying to build a construction business. See where I'm going? I am supposed to give myself up for my wife first. My love for my wife should be the purest love there is. It should be sacrificial. It should be sacred. Yet I give myself more to other things. Those other things are about my enjoyment, which really means I'm refusing to sacrifice what I want in order to make sure Laura gets the love she deserves and needs.

If this were the only verse about husbands in the entire Bible, it would be enough. It tells us all we need to know about our job as a husband. We are to love sacrificially so that our relationship to our wives paints a vivid, beautiful picture of how Jesus loved us and literally gave Himself as a sacrifice. My marriage to Laura has meaning. It has a purpose. Together we can be greater for the kingdom than we could have been on our own. Some people are called to singleness because in that singleness they are better for the kingdom than they would be with a spouse. If you are married, it's

God's intent that your marriage be a force for His kingdom here on earth. Husbands, this begins with you. Thank God for godly women who push through even when their husbands are failing miserably at leading the way.

Marriage is a lot like a machine. Let's compare it to a car. Your car can run when certain things are not right. But it won't run to its peak performance. Maybe the MPGs go down. Maybe it misfires on a cylinder and runs rough. Maybe it has a flat. There are routine things you can do to avoid these types of problems with your car. Marriage is similar. We need routine maintenance and check engine lights to let us know when something is not right. Husbands, it's your job to make sure the marriage is starting the right way. Just like in a car, there are obvious things you can't control. But think of yourself and your role as the battery and the ignition. The marriage starts with you.

We will never reach the level of perfection Jesus did, but the first step to being great as a husband, father and, just in general, a man is understanding that we are not enough on our own. We feel a lot of pressure to be everything to everyone, but Jesus is calling us to protect our marriage. Let down the wall of pride that keeps you from moving past this concept and start to put in the needed work. This means honoring your wife and/or family by respecting them as priority. You take care of your family first then start meeting the needs of others.

To The Wives - Laura
When I met Nick in college, I remember his circle of friends. All of his guy friends were lookers (hey, a girl's gotta be honest—birds of a feather flock together). I will salvage myself

by sharing that he was the fairest of them all. After all, he did get the girl (I'm not as shallow as I sound). I remember telling him before we started dating that I wasn't a prize to be won. My girlfriends and I refused to be seen as trophies, and if that was what he intended, he could keep fishing. I wasn't playing the game. Luckily, he wasn't either. My guy was respectful, smart, witty—and he loved Jesus.

More about our unusual love story later. Fast forward fifteen years, and I have twelve years' experience as his wife under my belt. Twelve years of experience, yet still a lifetime of learning remaining. Thankfully, when it comes to being a godly wife, an entire section of the Bible is dedicated to this very subject. The end of Proverbs gives wives twenty-one hefty verses as an example of noble living. Let me speak directly to you ladies for a moment. I want to peel back a few verses in Proverbs 31 that I have always tried to ignore.

"The heart of her husband trusts in her, and he will have no lack of gain" (Proverbs 31:11, ESV).

Okay, Proverbs says my husband should trust me. Check. My husband should have no lack of gain. No lack of gain? Gain of what? Digging deeper, I discovered that this so-called gain refers to his credibility. In other words, my husband should have no lack of credibility and respect with having me as his wife. When this clicked the first time, I had a mind explosion. Does that mean I actually should be a trophy? I felt restless. No, not a trophy. But I should actually make him feel proud. My character should bring him credibility.

Since we've already cracked this door, I'm going to swing it wide open. As she brought her husband "good, and not harm, all the days of her life" (Proverbs 31:12), so we should do the same. I know, I know, that's quite a high expectation. Nick and I both know that I am not a constant bundle of joy. I secretly enjoy making him simmer with my passive-aggressive silence. It's a good thing the Bible tells us to follow Jesus's example of love and not mine. Apparently, we aren't supposed to poke the fire. Instead, we are supposed to "think of ways to motivate one another to acts of love and good works" (Hebrews 10:24, NLT). Cheers to us wives who are trying to live out the Proverbs 31 virtues!

On countless days I give Nick my leftovers. As a matter of fact, I believe more often than not, I march through my day doing the mom thing and completely forget him. I fall asleep before asking about his day. I forget to switch over the laundry that he's asked about four times. When he gets home, I'm like Oscar the Grouch because the kids have used up all my patience.

My husband gets the worst of me. The struggle is real. If I'm completely extended and exhausted, shouldn't my husband be the one who builds me up? If I am empty, shouldn't he be the one to fill my tank? Incorrect. My sinful heart wants to say, "Yes, girl, don't lift a finger. You've done enough!" This can quickly morph into a prideful attitude driven by entitlement. The Bible teaches us that God is the source of power, energy, motivation, and love. To serve our family, we must tap into God's power and stop pretending we can do it on our own. We will break. Maybe not today. Maybe not tomorrow. But relying on our own strength to be a Godly wife is a sinking ship.

Ladies, today can be a fresh start. Love your husband immensely and reflect on whether you are adding or taking away from the spark in your marriage.

Keep God on the Pedestal - Laura

One more tender story. Don't gag. It was 2005, and after text flirting, we agreed to give this a chance. We met at the fast-food restaurant, Krystal's (which I hated but refused to make a fuss). Despite the anticlimactic first date, we hit it off. Normal couples would take that as a good sign and continue dating. I, on the other hand, got all weird, and a few weeks later told him I needed space. By this point we had been crushing hard, and I was sure he wouldn't understand my reasons for such a request. You see, in all transparency, I had experienced a break up a few months prior and my heart hurt. I was afraid to fall for a guy and let him become my identity again. It was like God was telling me He needed to work on me a little longer before I gave my heart to Nick.

Sitting in the parking lot at my dorm, I told Nick I was too broken to invite him into my story just yet. To create boundaries, I told him I didn't want to talk to him or even see him for a while. I knew I could easily place a boyfriend on the pedestal God deserved to be on. God was the one and only one I needed on that throne. It was too risky to start a new relationship with my faith wavering. Call it a fast, call it a break, call it whatever makes sense to you. I call it God leaning in and setting up a solid foundation for the future that He knew was ahead of us.

Forty-six days and a whole lot of God stories later, with the coordination of my best friend and roommate, Jenna, Nick knocked on my dorm room door. There I stood, shocked in my penguin Christmas PJs, mismatched socks, frumpy hair and wide-eyes, accepting his flowers and gummy bears. He asked me out, I said yes, and the rest is history.

We believe that if we had not stepped back and slowed down, our relationship would not have worked out. Or it would have been very, very messy. Sure, that is a wild assumption. But Nick and I both grew tremendously during that time apart. I really believe God was working something out in our hearts so we'd be less likely to sabotage a good thing.

Whether you are married, single, or widowed, your relationship with God is just that. Yours. To ensure you have God-centered relationships, you must keep God on the pedestal. No relationship can replace God's role in your life. No one can complete you. If you've been doing it wrong thus far, it's never too late to surrender and ask God to help you realign your priorities. And if you've lost that loving feeling, ask God to rekindle the romance in your marriage and be willing to fight for the covenant you made.

Know Your Weaknesses - Nick

What's the secret to a long and healthy marriage? I don't know the magic sauce, but I do know that keeping God at the center is non-negotiable. Laura and I have had our tough seasons. It's true what they say—opposites attract. We are polar opposites in many ways, but somehow we fell in love and stay in love. For example, we handle arguments differently and still live to tell about it. God brought two sinful humans together who are trying to braid their two lives into one while pointing others to Him. Yes, read that sentence again. Grab the popcorn. It's been quite a show.

One of the most important places in life to practice the idea of loving fast and living slow is in relationships. Particularly in marriage. If you are reading this and are not married, please read on. Don't discount this chapter because you don't think it applies. These principles apply across a wide range of relationships. I've been married to Laura for over a decade as I'm writing this. I can think of countless times in the past (and present) that I have been quick to anger and quick to speak, slow to forgive and slow to love. Life is crazy enough without allowing disagreements to disrupt my marriage in an unhealthy way. Any kind of relationship takes work, but marriages take more than most. Add three kids to the mix, and time becomes a precious commodity. Tension can climb and patience thins, which just upsets the applecart even more. It's not easy living out the words David wrote in Psalm 4:4, NKJV:

> "Be angry and do not sin. Meditate within your heart on your bed, and be still."

My natural reaction to something that upsets me is to get angry and then let everyone else know about it. I'll give you an example from my younger years. Being an avid sports fan, I take winning and losing very seriously. I wish, at times, that I had not allowed myself to become so attached to the teams I am a fan of and that I didn't get bent out of shape when my team loses. During football season, my own wife would avoid being in the same room with me on a Saturday in the fall if the Georgia Bulldogs lost a game that day. Fortunately, UGA won a lot of games in those early years of marriage. Before we were married and early on in our dating relationship, it took a lot for Laura to get over how temperamental and fiery I was about things she saw as minor.

I had to grow up.

I needed to create boundaries personally and really lean in to the areas in my life that were keeping me from growing and becoming who I was meant to be. I still love my Bulldogs as much as ever. I am still just as passionate about winning and losing; however, now I guard my words and my heart from the attitudes and actions that aren't healthy.

If I got so angry at the end result of a football game that it was having a negative effect on my relationship with my, at the time, girlfriend and now wife, I certainly wasn't meditating on godly priorities. I needed to look around and see the truly important relationships in front of me. I was so caught up in the outcome of a college football game, from a school I never even attended, that I was rude to people I cared about the most.

All this to say, Laura and I are very different, as are most couples. Our differences are a beautiful thing, but they can also cause much conflict when we let them. When it comes to handling emotions, being emotional is not wrong in and of itself. It's not a sin to have a strong emotion. God is not more glorified if we are completely apathetic. We know this because Jesus is perfect, and He had a résumé of emotions. Jesus felt emotions from compassion to anger; He was troubled, greatly distressed, and sorrowful; He grieved, He was joyful, and He loved. Emotions are subject to the way we manifest them—through our actions. Your spouse did something to anger you? Great, join the club. Now we have the choice to react or respond. We talk about this a lot with our kids. When we see what triggers their anger, we coach them through the proper ways to respond to those feelings. Sometimes our kids' reactions involve golf clubs being thrown through windows (okay, that only happened once), and that is, dare I say, not a proper way to respond.

As David encourages us to "be still" in the earlier verse, his words are another reminder to slow our mind and words. Think about the quick quips, dramatic sighs, exasperated eye rolls, and petty body language you may be sending your spouse's direction. At that moment, you are giving power to the Enemy. The Enemy wants nothing more than to disrupt something that can point others to God. Marriage was created by God. Sure, we get a tax write-off and a great reason to throw a party, but our celebration is not why Satan wants to destroy marriages. We can see God's plan for marriage in Matthew 19:4-5:

> "'Haven't you read,' He replied, 'that at the beginning the Creator 'made them male and female,' and said, 'For this reason a man will leave his father and mother and be united to his wife, and the two will become one flesh?'"

Again in Genesis we read, "It is not good for the man to be alone." What about when God created Eve as "a helper comparable to him [Adam]" (Genesis 2:18)? And blessed them with the words, "be fruitful and multiply" (Genesis 1:28)? Marriage is vital to the design of creation, so of course it makes sense that the Enemy wants to sabotage it!

To love fast and live slow in marriage is to give your spouse the best of you.

CHAPTER THREE

Then Comes Baby in the Baby Carriage

"No discipline seems pleasant at the time, but painful.
Later on, however, it produces a harvest of righteousness and
peace for those who have been trained by it"
(Hebrews 12:11).

It seems natural to move from talking about marriage and the principles that help make it run smoothly to talking about parenting. That's because many principles that help maintain a healthy marriage also help us to be good parents. In the same way, many of the mistakes that I (Nick) make that hurt my marriage can be the same blunders I make in parenting. Being a husband to Laura is the highest honor I have in this life. My marriage is the gift God gave me to best reflect Him to the world. But following right on the heels of Laura are our three amazing kiddos. I couldn't wait for each of them to be born. I was probably that expectant dad who annoyed everyone, talking to everyone that would listen about all the things I wanted to do and be as a father.

First-Time Parents - Nick

On July 22, 2012, Laura and I had a fairly normal day. I was home for a brief weekend before heading back out of town for another week of work. My job at the time required a lot of out-of-state travel, and I found myself living in hotel rooms more than in my own bedroom. Laura was 37ish weeks pregnant with our first child, and I was about to leave for one more five-day trip.

On this particular Sunday, my work called to cancel my work project, so we were delighted not to rush to the airport. To make the most of our newly open schedule, we thought there could be no better time than now to squeeze in the recommended tour of the maternity ward in the hospital. On the way home, we stopped for an impromptu date at Outback Steakhouse. That meal, that night, those smells, our conversations—it was a great night, and one we will always remember. Even though we were broke as a joke, we ordered whatever we wanted. I had wings and a bone-in ribeye. We also shared a blooming onion—duh! Laura drank about 37 gallons of water, accompanied by 37 trips to the ladies' room. I'm not sure what she actually ate for dinner, but everything else is still quite vivid.

Then her contractions started (must have been the blooming onion). Sporadic yet painful, the contractions were noted, and we headed home. The next thing I remember was Laura waking me up around 3:30 in the morning to tell me we were headed to the hospital. When I got up, I noticed that the entire house was spotless and smelled fresh. I was packing a small bag (I know, ladies, I should've already had that ready), trying to get out the door, when I realized Laura had never gone to sleep. She was doing that "nesting" thing that pregnant women do, so she had ninja-cleaned our entire house in a couple of hours while I was sleeping.

Besides the baby being a few weeks early, the rest of the story is pretty typical. All of the details are etched into my memory because of the magnitude of what was about to happen. I eagerly awaited the moment that our firstborn would light up the room. When I first heard his cry and saw his squished face, I felt fear, joy, and tears in an instant. It was the strangest feeling in the world.

I felt fear because he was more red than I imagined and not breathing yet. I know now that all babies enter the world like that. But I was a rookie, so that lasted for a short moment. And this fear was followed by the fear of "How in the world do I protect and raise this child?"

Then a strange, fresh emotion weighed on my chest. Sadness. I knew this moment was fleeting. I knew the greatness of what I was experiencing would not last forever. I did not want that feeling to go away. In David Lomas's book *The Truest Thing about You*, he speaks of the reason that there is often a sense of sorrow in the happiest moments in our lives. He says:

> We think such moments should last forever. The wise writer of Ecclesiastes said that we have eternity written on our hearts. It's in these moments that we are most aware of that. When we feel such longing, we're embodying a truth of Scripture: we are made for another world. With our very emotions and feelings—with the very firing of synapses in our brains and with the very secretion of chemicals in our neural pathways

– we are testifying to the truth of Scripture.[4]

I can truly say that the birth of our first child was a milestone in my development as a man and protector. God chose me to be a father. Even with the nurses in and out, beeps and IV cords flowing every which way, it was truly one of the most live slow moments of my life. All time stood still as I stared at this little boy who would rely on me to teach him how to become a good man.

All of the emotions I felt the day I became a father still ring true today. Fear, smiles, and tears rotate themselves, depending on the season we are plowing through. I believe there are many right ways to parent kids. I thought I knew what I was going to do and how I was going to do it. Yet now being in the trenches, I'm shocked at how hard this parenting thing truly is.

In the Trenches - Laura

I love Nick's recap of becoming first-time parents. It's refreshing to relive nostalgic memories. Far too often we don't live slow enough to recap earlier chapters in our lives. When is the last time you sat back and recalled a live slow moment with your family? We define a live slow moment as a place in time where you intentionally experience that moment with all five senses (or as many as applicable). You don't hurry through it to get to the next best thing. You embrace it and allow parts of that moment to recharge your battery. Is it harder than you imagined to vividly paint the senses of special memories? It is for me too. Because life is fast. Life is noisy. And we often find ourselves in "fight or flight" mode.

Speaking of fight or flight, one morning a few years ago

when my oldest had already proclaimed his passionate dislike of me and it wasn't even 10 o'clock in the morning, our middle son stepped out of the pantry with a handful of Oreos as a reward for pooping in his pull-up (might I add, this is not something we reward). Our six-month-old had just cried herself to sleep on the dirty living room floor. I was obviously winning at this mom thing. This particular morning several strong (opposing) personalities paraded around my feet, and I knew I needed to grab ahold of some love ... real fast. In an attempt to maintain control and peace, I threw open the back door and commanded the boys to go play outside. Their little feet scurried out the door like a stampede.

Easy enough.

I told myself to take a deep breath. Check.

I tried my best to handle the stress in love. Check.

Now where is my caffeine? Found it. Check.

The tempo in the house changed immediately. Sending them to adventure land in the backyard brought the decibels in the house down to an almost silent level. Pleased with how I had prevented problems that kept WW3 from erupting, I poured myself some hot water for my tea. A few moments passed before I heard the splashes against the window. I looked out to see two skinny-dipping little boys bursting into laughter, causing a ripple effect of giggles under my breath.

Internal monologue: *Okay, I got this. It could be worse. A few hiccups, but I am back in control.*

SPLAAASH. Followed by screaming.

Before I could swallow that last sip, my oldest son dunked his brother under the water and held him there. What felt like the same millisecond, I banged on the glass door and yelled at the top of my lungs. Wide eyes looked up, realizing that no white lie would allow him to weasel out of this one. He was caught red-handed. I stormed out in pure rage. Once I ensured that everyone was safe, I yanked the culprit out of the water with one arm like the Hulk. My emotions registered somewhere between "Why did my three-year-old think that was funny?" to "Why does my five-year-old constantly push boundaries?" to "I bet every neighbor wants to call child protective services based on the drama behind their fence each day."

I was angry. I was beyond annoyed. I just wanted five minutes to eat breakfast (I still needed to make toast because the guilty trio had eaten my three previous pieces). Now it was 10:13 a.m. How could this be? I had eight more hours until Nick got home from work, and I was already ready to tap out. Jesus, take the wheel. And while You're at it, would You drive my kids around for eighteen years and bring them back when You're done?

I kid. I kid—sort of. But do you ever feel like you've put your best foot forward and it's just not good enough? Becoming a Godly parent is like getting dunked under water. When you're dreaming about parenthood, you think you have everything under control. But after a few moments, you start to realize your limitations. You start to panic. Where is right side up? I wasn't trained for this. I need a breath of fresh air.

You can read all the parenting books, volunteer at vacation Bible school at your church, and babysit the neighborhood kids, your nieces, and your nephews, but you will never know how to parent your child until you are fully immersed. It's pleasant and it's risky. Unlike parenting, swimming allows you to take a quick dip and then dry off. But parenting is a lifelong experience. And I'm not sure about you, but I cannot swim for 18+ years straight. If I relied on my own strength and endurance to paddle these arms and stay afloat amongst waves and wind, I'd soon grow weary. Our human stamina will eventually run dry, and our tenacity as parents can only carry us so far. To raise Godly children, we need a Lifeguard. Thankfully I know where to find Him.

Teach Them to Swim - Nick

Perhaps the greatest parenting mistake I have made so far was to rely on myself to get the job done. If I looked to other parents and simply copied and pasted their admirable parenting styles, I'd miss the chance to raise my family in the unique way God made them. He did not give us a clear rule book or how-to guide. Wouldn't that have been nice? God does, however, give us the foundation to build upon when it comes to parenting guidance. Since He gave us the Ten Commandments, why couldn't He have given us a checklist for "Ten Ways to Ensure Your Child Will Do Everything You Say." I believe God did not do this because He doesn't want us to focus on the legality of child rearing. He wants us to raise our children as He raises us.

As you know by now, it's impossible to walk through life without facing adversity. As a matter of fact, adversity is a part of God's plan. Just as parents don't want their children to grow up feeling entitled or spoiled, our Heavenly Father knows the best way to raise us includes enduring suffering.

"Consider it pure joy, my brothers and sisters, whenever you face trials of many kinds, 3because you know that the testing of your faith produces perseverance. 4Let perseverance finish its work so that you may be mature and complete, not lacking anything" (James 1:2-4).

It's hard to watch your child go through trials and tribulations. I can recall a day when I witnessed our oldest son being bullied by older kids in the neighborhood. I about lost it. Laura reminded me that I am not allowed to fight a ten-year-old. As parents, we don't purposely put our children in the line of fire, but as they grow and mature, our godly response should be to let the trials test their faith...which will produce perseverance...which will grow into maturity... which will make them wise.

Another way that Laura and I are choosing to mimic God's parenting style is to lead with grace and correction, not law and punishment. It's the whole love fast thing. Our kids are strong-willed, and one is on the autism spectrum. We've had to unlearn all we thought about discipline and re-learn new methods based on the neurodiversity living under our roof.

We work really hard on correcting things that affect character and moral excellence. The things that are annoying or simply an inconvenience can be addressed differently. We are trying to use the words "correction" or "consequence" instead of punishment. Jesus already paid the punishment for our sin. All of it. Because of Jesus, my children don't have to pay for the price of being sinners. We hope to teach them that God doesn't punish them for being a sinner. Quite the opposite. He loves them. He forgives them. He washes them clean. That's grace. And if my kids learn nothing else from their upbringing, I want them to know they will fall down, but they are free to get back up because of God's never-ending grace.

Everyone Makes Mistakes - Nick

We want to fill our home with love, laughter, and humility—as do many of you, I am sure. We want our home to be a safe place to figure things out, solve problems, get better, and grow. Part of our bedtime routine with our children is to read a book. Recently we've been reading a book called *Everyone Makes Mistakes*, and even though I never want my kids to put gum in their sister's hair or paint her face with permanent markers like the character in the book so eloquently does, the underlying message is that you can always make a comeback. Just because you fail once or twice or five hundred times, that doesn't make you a failure. It makes you in need of a Savior.

Having consistent expectations for your child to be respectful, obedient, and kind certainly aligns with God's teachings. To love your child is to correct them so they will be ready to do whatever God has assigned for them (1 Corinthians 7:17). We must be patient in the aggravating moments—even in the small things, like when my littles come chanting "DADDY! DADDY! DADDY!" without giving me a chance to respond. Perhaps those chants come just as I have settled down in front of the TV or when I'm working on my car. When I respond with patience and answer their questions delicately, I imagine that is how Jesus responded to the little children running to Him when the disciples tried to shoo them away (Matthew 19:13-14).

Be fully present. With confidence, know that you showed your kids that wherever they are, you will be all there. Put the phone down. It's hard, and I still fail time and again, but I am aware of it now. I wasn't for a while. I think I became more aware of it when my second son was born. We try to carve

out specific times each day to be present with the kids indivi-
dually. I love having one-on-one time with them. My hope is
that it will show them they are valued, I am proud of them,
and they are safe to learn and grow when they are with me.

**To love fast and live slow in parenting is to raise your
kids like God raises you (with patience and forgiveness).**

CHAPTER FOUR

Your Born Identity

"But our citizenship is in heaven. And we eagerly await a Savior from there, the Lord Jesus Christ" (Philippians 3:20).

I (Laura) am pretty forgetful—not like, "Oh, what was your name again?" forgetful, but "Oops, I forgot my ID" after arriving at the airport forgetful. The pun is not lost on me that I don't even remember if I've always been this way or if it's surfaced since having children. I'm sure it's both. What I do know is that it is a frequent issue.

Rewinding back to high school, I would sometimes torture my sister by forgetting to put her borrowed (more like stolen) clothes back where I found them. Or in college, after I locked my keys in my car thirteen times, Triple A sent a letter of cancellation to my mom because I had exceeded our family's limit of roadside assistance for the year. Or decade.

Oh, it gets better.

I've been known to send Nick to the doctor with one of the kids, only to learn that the appointment was the next week. When my to-do list is a mile long, I tend to black out and wake up at the end of the day in disappointment that I did not conquer the world in 24 hours. I used to be a detail mogul. Now I'm lucky if I remember to close the garage door when I leave home.

Not being keen on details, triple checking that I had my wallet was not on my agenda as Nick drove me to the airport for a work trip. I'll tell you a secret (don't tell Nick). As we pulled out of our neighborhood, I thought, "I hope I have my wallet. Should I check my bag? Nah, I should be good." After all, I had my phone in hand and my luggage in the back—all of the important things, except proof of identification.

If you are a frequent flyer, have flown once or twice, or are even slightly aware that giant aluminum cylinders with wings transport cargo from one destination to another, you likely know that having your ID to get past security and board the plane is of the utmost importance. But me—nah, I'll just wing it.

As we pulled up to the crowded terminal drop off, I felt it was finally time to confirm that I had all necessary travel documents. I searched my book bag (my catchall and black hole). Not in there. I look on the floorboard of the car. Nowhere in sight. Opened the glove compartment. Negative. At this point, Nick had unloaded my carry-on bag from the trunk and became suspicious that I was in the act of pulling a "Laura."

"What are you looking for?"

Without making eye contact to own up to my shame, I kept my head down, searching again through the black hole. "My wallet," I slurred.

Admitting faults is never satisfying. My defense mechanism is to deflect frustration and belittle the consequences of my oversight. My internal monologue was less forgiving:

Well, Laura, you really screwed this one up. Worst case scenario is you don't go on this trip. Best case scenario is you meet the nicest Terminal Security Agent (TSA) on the planet, and he or she escorts you through security, approves your claim of identity even without proof, and you are able to slide into your 37A seat just in time. I had to get out of the car and face the consequences—good, bad or ugly.

It has been said that it takes 10,000 hours to become an expert at something, and I'm pretty sure I was on the brink of crossing into the expert ball dropping category. I'm a pro. That day at the airport I chose to remain hopeful that the latter was bound to happen. I got out of the car, keeping my phone glued to my hand because statistics were high that I'd misplace that too. I marched into the Hartsfield-Jackson Atlanta airport at early thirty that Thursday (the largest and busiest airport in the world, mind you) with no wallet, no ID, and no validation of my identity, and I asked them to board me on a four-hour flight across the country with 192 other passengers. Cake walk.

Just kidding. Security and safety policies for airlines are not something you can schmooze your way through. It's black and white. A line in the sand. And if you bat your eyes or plead too strongly, you're deemed a bit suspicious, thus decreasing your chances of ever stepping foot onto the airplane. My plan of redemption was to remain patient and grateful to anyone who helped me right my wrong. Nick remained close by, circling the airport until he got word of the final verdict.

Our Born Identity - Laura

Identity is an interesting thing. We are born with a definitive identity. We are either male or female. We are immediately a

citizen of a country. We have unique, one-of-a-kind finger-
prints. We are assigned a 9-digit numerical code that tells the
government who we are and how to find us. These things are
decided for us. Certain parts of our identity are outside of
our control and ultimately crafted by God's design. However,
for most of us, who we are, where we end up, and our per-
ceived self-worth are born (or reborn) in the decades after
our birth.

As I walked through the airport that day, I was a nobody.
I didn't exist. I couldn't prove who I was, and not one airport employee was allowed to take me at my word. For the
first time ever, I envied those being cattle called through the
security line. Being advised to wait for a TSA supervisor for
further screening, I rehearsed how I'd plead my case. I was
ready to prove my identity. Put me on the stand.

How often do we find ourselves defending who we claim
to be? Taking it personally when someone questions our motives or integrity? After all, if they really knew you, they'd
know you are a pretty good person overall. If they spent time
with you, watched how you serve your family, witnessed your
generosity, or knew about the project at work you just slayed,
then they'd observe and conclude you weren't all talk. Merely
reciting your résumé of "good person" characteristics does
not give you a "get out of jail free card" when you make mistakes. On the contrary, people decide to trust you when your
self-proclaimed identity aligns with your background check.

There was zero chance I could bypass airport security
protocol by stating how trustworthy I am or promising
never to make this mistake again. Not a chance. Instead, they
walked me through an intense screening and background
check, searched all my bags, and executed a very thorough

pat down. And of course, I complied. I waited patiently for their next instruction and began feeling at ease. After all, if the final ultimatum boiled down to my being the real Laura Mendenhall, then I had nothing to hide.

I imagine this is what people might feel like if they were waiting at the pearly gates to get into heaven. Those who felt it necessary to plead their case and defend their identity by listing out a résumé of good works would seem suspicious. "Look, let me in! I'm a good person. I know I've made a few mistakes, but I won't do it again."

God is a loving God…a gracious God…a forgiving God. But no amount of good deeds or smooth talk will bypass the one requirement to enter into heaven. God's security screening is simple. Your name is either written in the Book of Life (see Revelation 20:11-15), or it isn't. No negotiation. No exceptions. End of story.

That requirement may at first seem bleak. Wow, God. Really? That cut and dry? Coldhearted!

On the contrary, God has given us (mankind) every chance to lay down our life and pick up a new identity: an identity that says, "I believe Jesus is the Messiah, that He lived a sinless life yet took on the punishment of sin with a horrifying death on the cross. He rose from the dead three days later, and to fulfill prophecy, He gave us the ultimate gift of the Holy Spirit after He ascended into heaven. That Holy Spirit can live in our hearts, wash away the death penalty we deserve, and will teach us to live more like Jesus throughout our lifetime."

Now that's the identity I want!

When I get to heaven, there will be no identity crisis for me. I will have nothing to hide, not because of anything super-duper awesome I've done but because I felt that nudge on my heart and believed that He's the real deal. I now enjoy that feeling that says the only life worth living is a life with Jesus in my heart. I accepted that gospel as truth. God has written my name in the Book of Life. And it can never be erased. That's who I am. I am Laura Mendenhall. I am His.

I'm His. Now what? - Nick

So what happens when we put our trust in Jesus and things look the same as they did before we knew Him? Are we really saved? Does God really help me? Is there a real heaven and hell? Can we really trust Him if we don't feel different today than we did yesterday? These are just a few of the questions that come to mind when I think about my unreliable, sinful nature. How can I be identified with Someone I am so far from representing well? Thankfully, the truth of the gospel always trumps my feelings. The greater news is that we are not the first to feel this way and we will not be the last.

I was born and raised in church. My family was at church every time the doors were open. My dad was a minister of music, and my mom was in the choir, a Sunday school teacher, and a leader of what the Southern Baptists used to call G.A.'s for Girls in Action. My older brother and I were in R. A.'s (Royal Ambassadors) and basically every other program that existed for kids. I knew all of the right answers to the common questions about the Bible or Christianity. I could quote a handful of verses that most people (even non-churchgoers) could quote back then. In many ways, my identity was wrapped in the church.

I played some sports and had other hobbies, but for the most part I was that church kid. When I was about six, my best friend, Mitch, wanted to walk down the aisle between the church pews to "pray the prayer of salvation" so that he could be baptized. I figured now was as good a time as any for me to do the same thing. The pastor came to our house and talked with my brother and me. We confirmed it was time to do this, so walk the aisle we did. Dunked under water, we were. Members of the church, we became (not sure why I just decided to write like Yoda speaks).

Relief flooded my mind that everything was now good: I could die, and I would go to heaven. That was all it meant to me at that point. I did not understand anything about identity, sin, or life change. I was six. The worst thing I had done in my life was throw a rock and break the window of my dad's 1986 Toyota Corolla.

Did I believe in Jesus back then? I believe I did. Lots of people believe in Who Jesus is and even what He did in dying. But I think a lot of the people who would say they believe in Jesus would deny the need for a completely new identity in Him.

The summer between my high school freshman and sophomore year, real change began to take place. I'm not sure what started the shift in me; it was likely a combination of things. It was the first time I began to feel that God was genuinely moving in my life. At the time, I knew I felt a new sense of connection with the Jesus I had always claimed to know. This is when I began to understand what being saved really meant. God was changing me from the inside, and it wasn't because I was trying to win approval from those closest to me. I began to see my need for Jesus like I never had before.

My salvation was, what I like to call, progressive. Jesus

began changing my identity a little bit at a time. I began to understand what it meant to be lost and in need of a Savior. The older I get, the more I appreciate grace. Even being in a relationship with God for decades, I still screw up all the time. I am thankful I am not identified by my mistakes. My identity is in God's grace.

Too many people are walking around hollow inside, hoping that one day they will find the identity God wants for them or that they want for themselves. If that is you, take a deep breath and say this out loud: "Therefore, if anyone is in Christ he (she) is a new creation. The old has passed away; behold, the new has come" (2 Corinthians 5:17). Are you in Christ? If so, immerse yourself in that identity. But how do we do that when we screw up so much?

By understanding that our identity is no longer characterized by our fallen nature but by our redeemed nature. And by owning the identity in Jesus and humbling ourselves, and allowing the God Who saved us to change us. He changes us even when it's hard and even when it goes against all that the world says is good and acceptable. You no longer have to strive to prove your identity or worth; God has claimed you. You are His.

To love fast and live slow is to stop striving to prove yourself and instead surrender to who you are in Christ.

CHAPTER FIVE

Your Place in Community

"I long to see you so that I may impart to you some spiritual gift to make you strong—that is, that you and I may be mutually encouraged by each other's faith"(Romans 1:11-12).

I (Nick) still remember sitting in my social psychology class at the University of West Georgia in 2003. My professor kind of looked like a half turtle, half man. Or something from a cartoon anyway. But he was a great teacher and was really passionate about his work. I remember the day I first learned about collectivism. He was adamant about this subject, as if it were something that deeply affected or moved him. Now I understand why.

We We live in a society that values the individual above all else. Well, at least if you are reading this in the context of Western culture, it's more than likely true for you. One way Merriam-Webster defines *individualism* is "a doctrine that the interests of the individual are or ought to be ethically paramount," and this seems to be a pretty accurate definition of how we live. If you think about it, you would probably agree that, as a general rule, we are very much focused on ourselves more so than on others. From the time we are born, our world is pretty much all about us.

If you came from a traditional home life where mom and dad were both present, your existence was probably welcomed. You had a nursery designed just for you with colors that your parents thought would be great for you. There were showers thrown so that you would have clothes, diapers, pacifiers, bottles, strollers, and car seats. Countless dollars were spent getting ready for your arrival. After your arrival, you were the center of attention for the foreseeable future. You know how the rest goes. I don't want to take for granted that some of you may not have had the same charmed life I did, but a large majority may relate to what I am describing.

I'm not downing the practice of loving children into this world in a big way, but when we are not careful, the mentality of self-centeredness becomes part of who we are. We focus so much on ourselves that we neglect to notice the world around us and its needs. Not only that, but we are often not even taught the value and necessity of community and living with a sense of togetherness.

On the flip side of individualism is a culture of collectivism, not the idea of communism or liberalism in the political sense. If you research collectivism, you will find lots of negative ideas; this discussion is not about that type of collectivism but about the mentality that our lives are intertwined with our community and we as individuals have a responsibility to help maintain and improve the world around us and beyond. My professor was especially passionate about this type of collectivism. He was convinced that the level of individualism in our culture would eventually lead to a separateness that could destroy empathy, sympathy, and most importantly relationships that are necessary for a healthy, functioning society.

Humans were created to live in community. We need our surrounding world to make us better, and our surrounding world needs us to become better. We are not meant to have a parasitic relationship with our community and surrounding world. What happens when we begin to live the way we are intended to live in the context of community?

I love to read the first few chapters of the book of Acts. We get to see the foundation of the church being put into place. We get to see a picture of what God intended life to look like within our communities. In Acts 2, what happens within the local community after people meet Jesus is broken down for us:

> "Every day they continued to meet together in the temple courts. They broke bread in their homes and ate together with glad and sincere hearts, praising God and enjoying the favor of all the people. And the Lord added to their number daily those who were being saved" (Acts 2:46-47).

Some truths in Scripture grab my attention, and this is one of them. Getting a word picture of the love and unified mindset of the believers helps us to see that God intends us to live that way. Maybe we can't go out and sell everything we own or give all we have to someone in need, but our cultural context is different now than it was then, at least for most of us. Even so, I do believe God wants us to live with that kind of abandon towards our possessions.

Stuff is not bad. God created fun, and I love fun as much

as anyone. But are we willing to part with a particular way of life in order to see the lost come to know Jesus? Are we willing to put off personal desires to have the ability to help others in need? Do we see needs without people having to point them out? And are we quick to try to meet those needs when there is opportunity to do so? That's what we see in the early church. That is what I want to see in my life and what I hope you want to see in yours.

Looking back at my life in college, I remember watching other students who were trying to live and love like this. I had friends that would hop in a car and go help with disaster relief without any planning or notice (we had a few hurricanes hit the nearby coast during those years). They did it because they genuinely cared about people in need. But I stayed on the sidelines. It's not that I didn't care or that I didn't want to help. In fact, I genuinely did, but I had other priorities, some of which were my trying to be a responsible adult. To be honest, some of the people that were "abandoned" to the needs of others were, in reality, irresponsible with their time. A few of them might still be working on their degrees. It's important to be aware of the responsibilities God has given us while also being acutely aware of our community around us. Getting serious about connecting with others—by doing life with them, creating deep friendships, and keeping your door open for new fellowship—is one of the real ways God intends for us to make a positive difference in the world. Collectivism isn't a fairy tale; I believe Acts chapter 2 is still possible.

Seeing the Needs of Others - Laura

Nick makes friends easily. I, on the other hand, am more introverted and use that as an excuse. Back in 2011, I actually told

Nick, "I don't need friends." We had recently moved to Florida to help launch a church, and my job in Georgia graciously allowed me to keep my position and work from home (I traveled most of the time anyway, so they were used to my not being in the office). Nick and I were both born and raised in Georgia. By born and raised, I mean since first grade. Before first grade my family lived in Germany (Army Brat).

Although we lived hours apart, God eventually merged our paths together (as you already know). In college, I met most of my lifelong best friends. I've always considered myself a friendly person, but making best friends hadn't come easy. In high school, I was obnoxiously involved in every possible extracurricular activity. To be precise, I was likely president of whatever club or team I participated in. If my name was on the roster, I'd eventually make a run for the top.

I was into cheerleading and dance. When the doors of the church were open, I was spearheading the youth group shenanigans. In spite of all of those extracurricular teams, clubs and groups, I still felt lonely. I was home with no one to hang with on the weekends. I was visible but not reachable. It wasn't until college that I began to feel the weight and void of living for myself. Up until this time, I had been plugged into a community but was still living for me.

When I planted roots and started doing what I love, leading Bible Studies and connecting with other women, I finally understood this idea of belonging. That was my safe space. A group of us gals got together every Thursday morning and studied the Bible together. Sometimes it was all study and no chat. Sometimes it was all chat and no study. What came of that intentional time was a great sense of belonging and trust. Those girls became family. We were real, raw, and non-judgmental. It blew my mind that I had been missing that aspect of community my entire life. And it didn't matter what they needed, I'd do it. If it helped them, it would be my pleasure. I desired to be a reliable friend.

After Nick and I got married and moved to Florida, I clung to my previous friendships and shut the door to new ones. I decided that even hundreds of miles away, I already had my co-workers, my college besties, and my family. I didn't need to find a local community. It was too risky. I had opened up to a small circle once already. Wasn't that enough? Nope. Jesus didn't give us the option of playing it safe when it comes to loving our neighbor. He made it very clear to consider others better than ourselves (Philippians 2:3), and it starts next door.

Nick, the wise one, says it's far too easy to live (even accidentally) with an "I can get by on my own" mindset. I hadn't a clue what it looked like to wake up in the morning eager to meet the needs of a neighbor. I woke up in the morning ready to tackle my to-do list and check off whatever item would give me the highest praise, the most credit, or the fastest results. Yes, this sounds embarrassingly prideful. I wasn't trying to be a narcissist, truly.

Our whole lives we are conditioned to think about ourselves first. I don't blame my parents, I don't blame my school, and I don't blame the media (okay, maybe just a little). I blame sin. We are humans. And when Adam and Eve thought they could put their desires above God's, sin changed the world. That prideful pattern has been on repeat ever since. Every time we have a choice to demonstrate love and compassion towards someone but we do a hard pass in the name of "this is out of my comfort zone" or "can I trust you?" or "maybe next time," we are hitting that same repeat button. Over and over and over.

I see a need, but is it really my responsibility?

I see a need, but today is just not a good day.

I see a need, but I don't know what to say.

I see a need, but I have needs too.

When I do hard passes on loving my neighbor and strengthening my relationship with them, I am saying my needs matter more than theirs. Jesus never did that.

For the person reading my admonition whose gut warns, "But what if something feels unsafe?" let me remind you that there are ways to connect and love your community safely and allow people inside your ten-foot radius. I am a rather petite person. Some would even say shrimp-sized (Pardon my random rabbit-trail thought: We recently went to dinner with our neighbors, and I was asked if I considered it cannibalism to eat shrimp. I laughed out loud). As a mom who frequently totes around three young kids, I will not put my family in a compromising situation. If the only needs you see around you involve sketchy scenarios and potentially dangerous environments, open your eyes wider.

To take ownership of any accidental narcissism you may be swimming in, reflect on the last time you met the needs of someone around you. Actually (I am feeling massive conviction), do we even know the needs of the people God has placed in our circles? I firmly believe the greatest gift you can give someone is your time. Friendships don't grow on trees. We must plant the seeds, water them, shine light on them, and in due time, we can all be living our real life Acts 2 storyline.

To love fast and live slow within your community is to open up and break bread together.

CHAPTER SIX

Your Piece in His Puzzle

"Do everything without grumbling or arguing" (Philippians 2:14).

I (Laura) always found it odd that we teach our emerging generation to have their career path chosen by the time they are 18-years-old. Sure, a few up-and-coming doctors and teachers know their destiny and run hard. But what about the others? Personally, I ran off to college and ended up changing my degree three times. After I got my bachelor's, I started a master's program and quit after one semester.

Nick and I would frequently joke, "What do you want to be when you grow up?" And he'd say he wanted to be retired. Unfortunately for him, God requires us to work. Actually, we don't see this as unfortunate at all. It was God's original plan. He assigned Adam the responsibility of tending and keeping the Garden of Eden (Genesis 2:15). Also, he was told to name all the animals. I am still quite impressed with that. Can you imagine having to come up with new words and names and then remember them all? I can barely keep my kids' names straight.

I remember that when I was little, Crayola was hosting a

"name this new color" contest. They encouraged kids from all over to submit names for the new shade of crayon to be put in the box. I wanted to be the chosen winner so badly. I think the name I came up with had 18 letters and 5 syllables. I didn't win. Crayola must have been looking for something a child could pronounce. Their loss. Adam definitely would have won.

Work has always been a part of God's plan—before and after the fall. Adam and Eve ate of the forbidden fruit in the garden that God planted. Then sin entered the world due to their bad choices. God told Adam that the ground he walked on was cursed and he'd have to toil for food all the days of his life.

> "Because you listened to your wife and ate fruit from the tree about which I commanded you, 'You must not eat from it,' Cursed is the ground because of you; through painful toil you will eat food from it all the days of your life" (Genesis 3:17).

I am not sure what work was like before the fall. Perhaps all of their food sprouted right in front of their eyes, perhaps they never felt too full, and perhaps kale tasted like brownies. I can only imagine. What I do know is that there is a clear difference between what work was before and after sin entered the world; otherwise, God wouldn't have associated "painful" as a consequence of work after the fall.

Thinking of the struggles of work can seem pretty depressing. Does that mean God wants us all to dislike our jobs and walk in constant shame because of the curse that fell on Adam and Eve? Are we living in daily punishment because it takes blood, sweat, and tears to put food on our table? Absolutely not. God doesn't intend for us to live in punishment. As we discussed before, we are not being punished. Jesus came, died, and paid the price for all of our punishment. Now our loving Father is simply training us to have a great work ethic, a positive attitude, and a Biblical perspective so that everything we do brings honor to Him, regardless of our occupation.

Nick loves watching a popular show on Discovery Channel called *Dirty Jobs*. It's about a guy who travels the world to learn about... you guessed it... dirty jobs. Some of his favorite episodes were the behind-the-scenes work life of a garbage collector, oil rig personnel, a dairy farmer, an embalmer and a pest control removal specialist. I can't think of too many fresh-out-of-high-school graduates who would jump for joy to be a pest control removal specialist. But that job is needed. And God makes sure His people have a variety of skills and passions in order for the world to operate according to His plan. We are one body with many parts. And each part (each career) is important.

> "If the whole body were an eye, where would the hearing be? If the whole body were an ear, where would the sense of smell be? 18But in fact God has placed the parts in the body, every one of them, just as he wanted them to be. 19If they were all one part, where would the body be?" (1 Corinthians 12:17-19).

When it comes to working, we tend to lump the idea of purpose and work together. I'm not trying to dumb down the significance of loving what you do as a job, but often we feel defeated when we don't have warm fuzzies all day, every day about our work. I'm the first to blame for encouraging this mindset. I used to adamantly believe (and teach) that if you weren't happy with your job, change it (which sends the message that people should follow their feelings over responsibility). Our feelings are unreliable and our feelings lie. Just last week I felt like it was a good idea to sleep in and skip my morning meetings. The tiny bit of extra sleep I gained was not worth it. The rest of the day was stressful, rushed, and full of backpedaling as I tried to justify my absence. Totally yucky.

Think of it this way: God knows the bigger picture. You are merely a puzzle piece. Oftentimes we wander from job to job, trying them out to see if our puzzle piece fits. We need the perfect spot—no itchy corners, off colors, or uncomfortable squeezing. We spend our whole life trying to fit into various puzzles, and if they don't feel right, then they must not be. We are convinced we are a lost puzzle piece without a home. Without a big picture to complete, we feel purposeless. We don't want to wander around alone as a solo puzzle piece. We need something to merge with. A bigger purpose. A secret map to align all our passions into one. We convince ourselves that if we don't have one solid pursuit, we are going to flounder our entire life. This sabotages God's creative plan. What if we have several causes or careers we are skilled and passionate about? Are we allowed to play on two teams? Nick dives into this next.

False Dichotomy - Nick

For years, I felt like there was this cut and dry line that separated the options I had in life. Honestly, it's still a lie I find myself believing at times: the idea that I either have to focus on my construction and remodeling business or that I have to leave that to focus on working in a church. That's just one example, one I'm wading through right now. Perhaps the metaphorical valley I am in is an excuse to feel stuck between two opposing mountains. I must scale one or the other. Never both. Or at least this is the falsehood I tell myself. The reality is that sometimes we have to trek through the valley a little further to find that custom pathway out. Sometimes we need to feel the freedom to do multiple things.

I remember when I was 23 years old and my world consisted of two options: get a job as a teacher using my degree or start looking for opportunities to be a student pastor in a church. Looking back, this false dichotomy was driven by fear of what others were going to think or say of me. A false dichotomy is just that. It's basically seeing a cut and dry line between two things and seeing only those two things. You can see no other options when in reality there could be countless options…that's why it's false. I'm not sure if I ever wanted to be a teacher. It seemed easy. I can assure you that it was not an easy job. I survived two years. Barely.

Teaching and church ministry were the two big mountains I was walking between, and in that moment I saw no other option. I ended up choosing both. Have you ever been passionate about multiple things? Torn between what will pay the bills versus what will fulfill your passion? You are not alone. What if there were a way to do both? I worked part-time in a church while being a full-time teacher and a coach of two sports. Even though I gave it my best go, after two years I never really found a passion for teaching in the school system. Perhaps I had to dip my toes in to know for sure. Life is like that sometimes. We need real field experience before we make a final decision. Are you willing to try something new in order to learn more about yourself?

I always admire people who don't seem to get caught up in false dichotomies. They never seem to question their choices or stress about what others think of the path they are on. These people are pioneers to me. They trek through the valley with resolve and vision. When there is a lack of vision and goals, we get knocked down by pressure to prove our significance. There is a constant burden to choose between secret door A or B. The truth is, you don't have to choose either. You can make your own door.

There are not usually true dichotomies in life. We make it seem that way because of our own insecurities or fears. Loving God and slowing down to appreciate what God is doing around you helps alleviate those distracting feelings. Here is a challenge for you. And for me. Stop focusing on all of your choices. Look for where God is working and start using your gifts and talents there. Spend your energy helping others because it's good, not because they have something to offer you. I believe that our truest passions and goals will become clear when we do those things well.

God's Gift to the World - Laura

Everyone wants to be a part of something bigger than themselves. I don't blame them. I do too. If only everyone would see how incredible we are. I mean, we are kind of a big deal, right? Companies should hire us with a salary offer double the going rate. Wouldn't that be nice? This, whether intentional or not, may be the lie we tell ourselves.

I am not here to lie to you though. These next few pages

may sting. This isn't going to be your grandma's pep talk. This isn't going to feel good. As a matter of fact, you might not like me after this. But it must be said.

Are you ready?

Here we go.

You are not that special.

I know most of us grew up hearing how special we were, and although our parents meant well, we need a wakeup call. We are not God's gift to the world. Jesus is. If we want to be special, we need more Jesus. The more Jesus we have within us, the more special we are. The more we are like Jesus, the more we have to give to the world. The bigger picture you are designed to fit into is God's plan. That's the puzzle into which you and I are meant to fit snugly. Imagine a giant, blank cardboard canvas and puzzle pieces cut out and separated but with no artwork or image connecting them.

What a difference it would make if we all decided to link our puzzle piece to His blank canvas and then trust the Artist to paint it however He wants. He makes the masterpiece, we do not. Would you be satisfied if He painted you beige? Or would you stomp your feet until you were bright orange and more noticeable?

When we seek work just so it will elevate us as the hero, it interrupts God's big picture. We work long hours and grueling weeks so that at the end of the day we receive the pay raise, the pat on the back, the promotion. These achievements are not necessarily bad, but if you are working in order to make your puzzle piece shinier, are you trying to draw more attention to yourself or to His overall picture?

There is nothing wrong with success. Nada. I love success. But be careful not to position yourself as the hero of your story. Live in humility. You can make your puzzle piece neon and cover it with glitter, but do it to bring more attention to His grace rather than your accolades. When the Creator of the universe, the King of all Kings and the Author of life and death invites you (a dirty, sinful, soggy, misfit puzzle piece) to be a part of His bigger story, then that's love. We are not owed a glorious story. He allows us to participate in His story.

Our gift back to Him is to show up to our responsibilities without complaining and do our due diligence with excellence. We are representing Him and His big picture, therefore, what we do matters, even the little details and the big decisions, the seen and the unseen.

"Humble yourselves, therefore, under God's mighty hand, that He may lift you up in due time"
(1 Peter 5:6).

To love fast and live slow is to happily fulfill the responsibilities God has given you right now.

CHAPTER SEVEN

Chasing Your Next Adventure

*"For He satisfies the thirsty and fills
the hungry with good things"* (Psalm 107:9).

I (Nick) think everyone has their own definition of adventure. To many of us born in the late 70s and early 80s, certain movies classify what adventure really looks like. In unison, let all the people say: the Indiana Jones film series and The Goonies! If you were born during that time period and do not still dream of finding a cave that leads to a pirate ship or an artifact of major significance, there might be something wrong with you. Seriously though, I still have this kid inside of me that holds out hope that one day I will have a real life adventure that rivals that of Indiana Jones or Mikey.

Not everyone feels the same way about adventure. I am an avid fan of all things adrenaline. There are few things I wouldn't try at least once. Sky dive? I'd give it a shot. Bungee jump off Victoria Falls? I'd love to. Tour with a band? Maybe one day if I'm good enough. I love to surf, snowboard, drive fast, and fly with my dad in his tiny four-seater Cessna 172.

I love hiking in the secluded mountains of North Georgia and Tennessee and primitive camping (even when it's in the teens outside).

One of my closest friends in the world is my cousin Evan. In 2008 he was getting ready to move to New York for school, so we decided to take one last guys' trip to camp in the Cohutta Wilderness in North Georgia. It was mid-February and had snowed the day before. A polar vortex or something like that was happening that made the high that particular day about 17 degrees Fahrenheit. Against my wife's better judgement and our parents' telling us we were crazy, Evan, our friend Derrick, and I loaded our backpacks, stuffed our bags with lots of extra blankets, and headed up Interstate 75.

We decided to start at a trail head we knew well. We calculated that we had a 5-mile hike one way to get to the Jack's River Falls, where we wanted to camp. This was destined to be our greatest adventure. Usually in the winter, the river is a little lower because there's not as much rain. This was important because the particular trail we had chosen has a river crossing, with no other way around it. We didn't care. Sign us up.

Water is already cold in mountain rivers, but imagine when it's 17 degrees outside. The crossing was 4 to 4 1/2 miles into the hike. We had made a late start, and it was going to be dark soon. As we arrived at the river, we realized that the snow from the day before had caused the waters to be higher than expected. Oops. Miscalculation. We were too deep in the woods now to turn back, and truth be told, the extra challenge added to the fun. We knew we didn't have a lot of daylight left, and it's not a good idea to set up camp when everything is dark, frozen, and wet.

What do three guys hiking in the wilderness do when they are tired, cold, wet, and nearly hypothermic? We walked barefoot through icy water, of course. We took off our shoes and scrunched our pants up above our knees to conquer this artic river as quickly as possible. We knew we would need a fire stat. We were tapping into our inner Mikeys, and nothing would stop us now.

The first step is always the worst. The sting that occurs in below freezing water is familiar and adrenaline-inducing. We all managed to get acclimated after our first few steps. Making headway with our packs raised above our heads, we knew the last steps were near, only six more feet to the bank. Balance is a challenge when you are as cold and tired as we were, not to mention the currents were particularly strong.

Then it happened. Evan lost his grip and slipped backwards. The current knocked him over and swallowed him whole into the slushy waters. Thankfully, he popped up pretty quick. We grabbed ahold of his gear and pulled him to the other side. Now the real Indiana Jones work started. We knew the immediate next step was to get him dry and warm. Our actions were urgent. We were miles from help, with no cell service and the sun already beginning to sink. First step, put on dry clothes. Second step, set up campsite. Third step, start the fire.

Our plans were panning out until we could not get a fire going. Our hands were numb, our energy was depleted, and no dry wood was in sight (remember, it had snowed the day before). To our disappointment, we never completed step three, perhaps the most vital step. We had no choice but to endure a fireless night. You can imagine that we experienced one of the longest and hardest nights of our life. We vastly underestimated how unpredictable, how cold, and how dangerous camping under those conditions actually was.

Spoiler alert: no one froze to death. We all survived, and to this day, it's one of our favorite memories together. In the morning we got the fire rolling and stayed warm and dry for the next two days. If you were to ask us if we'd do it again, the answer would be a resounding "YES!" We endured tough conditions doing something we love, and it was worth it. Are you an adventure junkie? Getting out in nature helps me slow down, and slowing down helps me think. Thinking helps me evaluate and appreciate what God has done in my life. For me, adventure is in my DNA. It's part of who I am and what makes me tick. For others, adventure may not be quite as natural or appealing. God doesn't require us to have an adventurous spirit, but if He drags you six miles past your comfort zone, you should give Him a resounding "YES!"

When the Adventure Stops - Nick

Something in nature draws me. It soothes me and calms me in my most anxious times. The cool thing is that I love all types of nature. Some people love the mountains and hate the beach. Some love the beach and hate the mountains. I want to see and experience it all. I'd love to own a large sailboat and sail all over the place, maybe around the world, with my wife and kids. I tell people that God created me to love water. For as long as I can remember, this feeling has been in my heart. It consumes me at times, even to the point of becoming frustrated because I don't see any sailing escapades in my near future.

Have you ever wanted something so badly that you lost sight of the good things around you? The more I dream of sailing off into the sunset, the more defeated I feel because my life is not a daily dangerous storyline like "little boy" Nick had once envisioned. I suppose this could all sound childish. I do believe God put a hunger for spontaneity and unexpected fun in all of us, even if a tidbit. Mine is just on fire—pretty much all the time.

I think wanting an abundant life is a good goal. No, a great goal. God wants us to experience a rush of adrenaline even in the mundane. When we are in the middle of His will, that's the most alive we can ever feel. Living a life surrendered to loving Him and others is the most radical adventure I could ever stir up. What good is it for me to gain the world without ever pointing others to Jesus? What good is it if I write my own story but never appreciate the story God invited me into?

> "What good is it for someone to gain the whole world, yet forfeit their soul?" (Mark 8:36).

Have you ever noticed that a lot of people who have it all (or so it seems) are still miserable and depressed? A lot of it has to do with the chase. They chased hard with max ambition, but along the way they forgot to find joy in the journey. They arrive at their destination, open up the big bow-covered gift box in front of them, and peek inside, hoping to see everything they've ever wanted. Then a wave of disappointment deflates their excitement. What's inside still isn't enough. It still doesn't quench their deepest need and longing. If they stepped on others to get to their mountaintop or compromised their integrity on the way, a feeling of emptiness trumps the celebration. Such a shame. The same goes for chasing experiences. If you chase the gift instead of the Giver, you will never be satisfied.

Your life may be a constant adventure, but it will still seem boring if you take God out of the picture. We can get our blood pumping when we surrender our ambitions to Him.

> "'For I know the plans I have for you,' declares the LORD, 'plans to prosper you and not to harm you, plans to give you hope and a future'" (Jeremiah 29:11).

In the spirit of transparency, here is what gets my blood pumping these days: speaking to as many people as I can about our Love Fast Live Slow mission; telling even more people about Jesus; seeing my kids grow to be successful, faithful followers of Jesus; seeing as much of the world as I can; operating successful businesses with integrity; eating my way through Asia (Andrew Zimmern style); and owning a boat and, if possible, a place on the water.

At the end of the day, my number one goal is to use whatever God gives me to make Him known. Can I do that with a boat? I sure hope so. However, don't allow your need for speed and spontaneity to replace your appreciation of your Savior. He knows you and your audacious spirit. Say "YES!" to Him and then put on your seat belt because it's going to get wild.

When You Get What You Ask for but Regret It - Laura
When it comes to experiencing something that fuels your soul, everyone is different. I love to journal. I love to read. I love to dance. All of these activities are life-giving to me. It's not often that I chase after something that positions me as the life of the party. I am usually content, unless I fixate on

something then I am relentless. Sometimes to a fault. When I was in college, I pursued one of these self-centered adventures aggressively while superficially inviting God to join me, which led to disaster. I got what I wanted, and it broke me in the process.

The main deciding factor as to which college I would attend was whether or not I'd be able to continue my love for competition cheerleading. I was an okay cheerleader, but my thrill came from the choreography and dance part. Competing with my teammates to perfect a three-minute synchronized cheer, dance, and tumbling routine was right up my alley. Two weeks before I graduated from high school, I changed my college plans because there was a glimmer of hope that I could walk onto a team at a school two hours away. When I did my research, I discovered that this specific school had several national championship titles under its belt in my sport. From that moment forward, I was obsessed. It's all I thought about that summer. I wanted that championship.

While unpacking my dorm room that first week of college, I got a call from a friend who was already on the team. She said they were holding an open practice that day, and I had an exclusive invite to join them at a gym nearby. Excitement, fear, and doubt filled my head, but somehow I made it to the gym and had the courage to walk through the doors. Concrete seemed to fill my shoes as I lifted them onto the tumbling mat. Being shrimp-size, I was always the flyer (this is the girl who gets tossed around).

It was a blast. The practice went well, and I was invited to come back the following week. Me! Little ol' me! They wanted me to learn their routine as they started to train for the January national championship. Pinch me. I was sure this must be God showing off. As my freshman year of college unfolded, I was spending a generous amount of time with my teammates. They were kind, and I did all I could to mingle without compromising my values. You know, college stuff. Yet in due time, I became more and more uncomfortable with the party scene.

Simultaneously, I had classmates inviting me to a local Christian organization that had weekly gatherings and Bible studies. I had to decline most invites because my practices overlapped the scheduled events. Here I was, 18 years young, and I wanted to be in all places at all times. Sounds pretty typical. I had spent hours and hours visualizing what it would feel like to be accepted by the inspiring athletes on my team. What would it take? Yet no matter how much time I spent on the mat with them, I felt disconnected and uneasy. It seemed I'd have to change who I was to reach the level of acceptance that didn't come with mockery or passive inside jokes about my faith. And on the other side of campus, I had a community of like-minded people offering encouragement and belonging. This standoff was almost too much for me to bear. But I persisted. My parents had taught me right, and I wasn't a quitter. I had made a commitment to this team, and I would finish what I started. After all, I had obsessed over the chance to win the national championship, so it must be God's will, right?

Winter practice schedules came out as the big day was drawing near. I was growing weary, and the spunk that had enthusiastically led me to this experience began to fade. I prayed. I felt all kinds of backwards. I asked God something in words I never thought my lips could compose. I asked Him to undo this answered prayer. Maybe this adventure wasn't in line with His plan.

"God, please do something."

It turns out, when you surrender your plans, God can right your wrong. The very next week during routine drills at practice, it happened. Never in my wildest dreams did I think He'd fulfill His plans as creatively as He did, but He is God after all: Mr. Creative.

While doing a backflip, I dropped to the floor. As did my ego. As did my dreams of winning that championship. As did my fight with God. The fall resulted in a broken arm that had to be repaired with surgery. As I was lying on the mat in the gym that day, my teammates drew close, asking if I was okay. You'd think I might have felt panic, embarrassment, and fear, but instead I felt relief. A weight lifted off of me that I cannot explain. In my brokenness, I felt more peace than pain. I knew immediately that this accident was meant for good and not for harm. After a night in the hospital, I was discharged with a six-inch plate and six screws (and a rowdy scar) in my right arm that will forever be a reminder that God's plans are better than mine.

We all have special goals or dreams we'd love to see come to fruition. No one sets out to live a boring life. We all want adventure and a sense of excitement. We can easily convince ourselves that when the stars align, it must be God. But not every open door is meant to be walked through. God has a plan and a purpose in the quiet moments of your life. He wants you to live a full, abundant life—on His terms. Wait for God to ignite your next adventurous step.

To love fast and live slow is to let God be your one and only adventure Guide.

CHAPTER EIGHT

Chasing Your Bank Account

"I'm angry. Angry at God. Angry at my husband. Angry at myself. We've been down this road before, and I recognize the unfortunate potholes and wrong turns. Is this a punishment? What could we be doing better? Or are You playing games with us? Testing our faith?"

This was my (Laura) journal entry on the morning of October 2, 2018, when we woke up and had negative $14.95 in our bank account. Negative. In the red. No savings. No secret stash. All we had was some money piled into our retirement fund that was already astronomically below what was considered on track according to our financial advisor, whom, I might add, we had been hiding from in shame for months (sorry, Jason!). This was a new low.

We never set out to be total failures. It just came naturally. Kidding. God doesn't make losers. Yet it's hard to remember that some days. Why did we feel as if we were always playing on the losing team? One step forward, seven steps back. What was even more alarming was that according to our tax returns, we made quite a bit of money. The government enjoyed their hefty portion, and we should have had smooth

85

sailing with our middle-class income. Yet we found ourselves living paycheck to paycheck, zeroing out our accounts several times a month. It was a humbling and scary time.

Please know that I do not write these words from a strong place. I write these words with complete compassion and empathy for those who have hit rock bottom in their finances. It would seem easy to stand above those in need and say, "Just trust God. He always takes care of His people. He's taken care of me, see? So He will take care of you." That stings. To those who can't make their mortgage payment or worry about putting food on the table, it's not comforting to receive assurance from those who are sitting pretty.

We are not extravagant people. As a matter of fact, poor Nick has been talking about upgrading our TV for over a decade. A DECADE. In our living room sits the same 42" TV he bought before we were married...twelve years ago. I suppose that is considered a first world problem. Also, when it comes to our wardrobes, we are basic. Minimalists probably. We eat from the same maroon and hunter green dishes we received as wedding gifts (why I registered for a red and green color scheme is beyond me). Until recently, our furniture has been hand-me-downs. And our hobbies are few and far between.

Unfortunately, we walked into a Grand Canyon of debt when our oldest son required several medical procedures, tests, therapies, and surgeries not covered by our insurance. Little by little, those medical bills added up and swallowed us whole. We've been chipping away at that debt for over five years. It's a monster waving a clever finger at us, teasing us with compounded interest and late fees. I'm convinced this same monster continues to sabotage us with car issues, house repairs, and spontaneous bills that steal any extra cash we find to aggressively pay down debt.

Why do I feel angry at God? Is our debt justifiable because we had a sick child? What does God think of money? Why does He seem to give some people money and wealth with ease? And others not so much? Does He choose this ahead of time? Are we not faithful enough to deserve it? Or are we thinking of money the wrong way? If you've ever had those questions flow through your mind, you are a kindred spirit. Even in the middle of our own financial crisis, God promises never to leave us nor forsake us.

Persistent Widow - Laura

Fast forward to July 16, 2019 (the day I reread and edited this chapter). We zeroed out our bank account again. Every time our bank account zeros out, I grow numb. When it happened the first time, we were scared. When it happened the second, third…ninth time, I grew apathetic. Had God forgotten His promise to take care of His children? If He took care of the birds in the sky, could He not give us a little handout? I wish I had some magical story of how God poured out silver dollar manna from heaven into our bank account. More than anything, I had hoped my pleading prayers to God would result in waking up to a cash tree in our front yard.

My pastor has preached many times about prayer. One message in particular, based on the parable of the persistent widow, has stuck out to me.

"Then Jesus told His disciples a parable to show them that they should always pray and not give up" (Luke 18:1).

Jesus went on to describe a persistent widow who repeatedly went to a judge, asking for justice against an enemy. Apparently her plea was frequent because she wore that judge down.

"The judge ignored her for a while, but finally he said to himself, 'I don't fear God or care about people, but this woman is driving me crazy. I'm going to see that she gets justice, because she is wearing me out with her constant requests!'" (Luke 18:4-5, NLT).

Even this judge who had no care for God or reason to extend justice to this widow caved to her consistency. This next verse changed my entire perspective on prayer.

"So don't you think God will surely give justice to His chosen people who cry out to Him day and night?" (Luke 18:7).

Yes! Yes, He will. And it's in those words I find peace and hope. We hope you can as well. In the trenches now with our own money woes, albeit hard, our faith is being strengthened. If you are asking God for wisdom, a promotion, or debt forgiveness, approach Him like the widow approached the judge: day and night. And note, she was asking for something that aligned with God's will, justice. When we are asking God for His favor, we should make sure it's aligned with His will and not our own vanity. Remain persistent and faithful, trusting that God hears your prayers day and night.

Lightning would strike us if we claimed to have perfect money management skills. We could all improve in budgeting, saving, and giving. Agreed? Whether it's improving on where to spend or how to make more in general, handling finances is a lifelong journey. Can we agree on another thing? The Lord will provide. The Bible confirms that truth over and over.

> "So do not worry, saying, 'What shall we eat?' or 'What shall we drink?' or 'What shall we wear?' 32For the pagans run after all these things, and your heavenly Father knows that you need them. 33But seek first His kingdom and his righteousness, and all these things will be given to you as well" (Matthew 6:31-33).

> "And my God will meet all your needs according to the riches of His glory in Christ Jesus" (Philippians 4:19).

I still struggle with doubt. I struggle with fear and worry. Money problems trigger major anxiety for me. Perhaps that is obvious by the drama queen emotion spewed out in this chapter. My security has been dangerously dependent on the size of our wallet. The only place I can run to is His Word for constant reassurance. More often than not, I am like the persistent widow asking God for a miracle. I wouldn't ask if I didn't believe it was possible.

If He Feeds the Ducks, He Will Feed You - Laura
There is another passage from Luke that resonates with me. Once again God flexed His miracle muscle to teach me some valuable lessons.

"Look at the birds. They don't plant or harvest, they don't have storerooms or barns, but God feeds them. And you are worth much more than birds" (Luke 12:24, NCV).

I can tell you from personal experience that our God feeds His birds. Sometimes He even uses us to provide for His creation. When I lived in Carrollton, Georgia, I would spend a few hours a week journaling, overlooking a lake, and living slow at the local park. The park had a few fishing piers and picnic tables, as well as a grassy hill atop a small dam to filter overflow into the lake. I would park my car, grab a blanket from the trunk, and skip over to the grassy hill with a journal in tote. I'd sit cross-legged on the blanket and let the pen in my hand fill blank pages almost subconsciously. This routine would happen often, especially during weeks when I felt particularly stressed with school, boys, work, or life in general. It was my rescue. That dam became my refuge for all of the overflow I needed to filter from my life. When my friends were looking for me, they knew I'd be at the dam.

I was that dam girl. Okay, jokes aside. You get the point (yes, I'm still laughing at my own joke).

God met me there a lot. I don't believe we always have to pre-arrange our meetings with God. We can call out to Him, and He will be there: in our house, in the classroom, in the car, in the bathroom, or in the grocery store. It's one of my favorite attributes of God. But there is something special, and almost divine, about setting aside a place to talk with Him.

Since my chosen place was by the lake, little feathered

and webbed feet friends would swim to the shore awaiting a kind handout of food. I'd see families walk up to throw breadcrumbs to these ducks, and they'd gather almost immediately, as if they had heard a dinner bell ring. It was cute—until it wasn't.

On one particular visit, I had cleared my entire afternoon to vent in my journal. Maybe I needed more real life friends. Nah, I needed to vent without a peanut gallery commentary interrupting my flow. After finding a comfy spot at a shaded picnic table, I opened my Bible and started reading.

Right on cue, the ducks arrived. They usually stayed right at the shore line: safe space for them and safe space for me. I am not quite sure why I looked approachable this particular day, but the ducks were fiery. One duck (I'll call him Huey) inched his way out of the water. Once the others saw his courage, they decided to conquer the land as well. Two more ducks arose out of the water (let's call them Dewey and Louie, catching onto my DuckTales theme?) and shook their tail feathers to wring out the lake water. They knew what they wanted and made a bee-line to my picnic table. I imagine this is how bold we look when marching up to God, expecting handouts.

Bad news for Huey, Dewey, and Louie. I was empty-handed. I didn't bring bread, crackers, or snacks. What you see is what you get, little duckies. They persisted. Closer and closer they paraded in my direction. I'm not a Disney princess, so I have zero qualifications to talk to the animals. I was there to pray, read, and recharge, not to be annoyed by these ducks. I wonder if God is ever annoyed by our begging. I've pleaded for a lot of things in my life—some I'm glad He didn't give me.

I opened my Bible randomly to John chapter twenty-one. Even though I was distracted and eerily close to being attacked by my hungry acquaintances, I read on. And the God moments that followed still blow me away.

> "Jesus said to Simon Peter, 'Simon son of John, do you love me more than these?'
> 'Yes, Lord,' he said, 'you know that I love you.'
> Jesus said, 'Feed my lambs'" (John 21:15).

I've read this passage before. I've heard it in church sermons and knew the overall theme. But this time was different. This time it was like God was speaking to me from a megaphone in the sky: "Laura, you asked me to meet you here. Do you love me?"

Um, yes, God. I shook it off, thinking I must be crazy. *I'm hearing voices*, I thought. I kept reading.

> "Again Jesus said, 'Simon son of John, do you love me?'
> He answered, 'Yes, Lord, you know that I love you.'
> Jesus said, 'Take care of my sheep'" (John 21:16).

Without explanation my heart started pounding in my chest. I mean, I did pray for God to meet me here, but this couldn't be a real-time conversation, could it? That'd be too weird. I can be weird, but this was weird for me.

The feeling was relentless. I took a deep breath and considered for a moment if God was literally asking me to show Him my love via caring for sheep. "I don't have any sheep, God" (yes, I said this out loud).

"The third time He said to him, 'Simon son of John, do you love me?' Peter was hurt because Jesus asked him the third time, 'Do you love me?' He said, 'Lord, you know all things; you know that I love you.'
Jesus said, 'Feed my sheep'" (John 21:17).

But I don't have sheep. Sheep don't live at the lake. What is this all about? All I see are these snippy ducks. You want me to feed these ducks? I don't have any bread. Not a crumb. I felt like I was failing God: One because I was in denial of even having this moment and two because I had nothing to feed His ducks. This all seemed ridiculous.

Maybe the ridiculousness of the moment was the kicker. Maybe it was because He was the One Who needed to provide the bread. Maybe my striving to fix the problem was getting me nowhere fast. I was growing more frustrated that I didn't have what those ducks needed. Far too often I try to play God and think I can provide for my own needs. When ultimately, Who is the giver of all good things? God.

I needed to let God be God.

I smiled, nodded, and closed my Bible. My worries about bills, career, relationships, and any next steps all mattered little when I put God in His rightful place. He was the provider I could trust, the leader I could follow, and my stability when I felt shaky.

Even today, 15 years after meeting those ducks, they mean a lot to me. Just as you and I quack at God to answer all of our financial requests, He reassures us: "I got you. I know what you need. You show up to do your due diligence. And then trust me and let me take care of my creation."

93

"Look at the birds of the air; they do not sow or reap or store away in barns, and yet your heavenly Father feeds them. Are you not much more valuable than they? Can any one of you by worrying add a single hour to your life?" (Matthew 6:26-27)

As I grabbed my bag and headed to the parking lot that day, I noticed an older woman parked nearby with her windows open. Everything in me resisted turning around to say hi. I was a stranger. I'm an introvert. She probably wanted some peace and quiet. But that tug on my heart was steady, so I braved it.

"Hi, how are you?" I smiled.

"Oh, hi!" she lit up. "I'm okay, thank you."

"Such a beautiful day. I love this part of the park."

"Yes, I used to come here with my children. Now they've all moved away, and it's pretty lonely since my husband passed away earlier this year."

This tender woman was dealing with the impossible, and I didn't know what else to say.

She continued, "We used to come here to feed the ducks. It was special. I brought some extra bread. *Do you want to help me feed them?*"

"Wow. Actually, yes. Yes I do."

As if the aha moments weren't satisfying enough, God really drove His message home. God takes care of His creation. The ducks and us.

To love fast and live slow when you are in need is to pray day and night and let God be God.

CHAPTER NINE

~~~

Chasing the Leader

"I am the light of the world. Whoever follows me will never walk in darkness, but will have the light of life." (John 8:12).

I (Nick) never set out to be a good follower. You don't see posters saying, "You can be a follower!" "Followers are created, not born!" "Work hard; become a follower!" Every message that saturates our minds screams that in order to win, you must lead. You follow, you lose. Leaders are the champions. Followers are second. And if you're not first, you're last.

What if we have it all backwards? Leadership is definitely seen and celebrated throughout the Bible: Abraham, Moses, Gideon, Peter, Paul, just to name a few. These men were greatly influential and foundational throughout the Bible. Their common denominator? They were exceptional followers. It's true, the better they followed, the better leaders they became.

Follower is defined as "a person who moves or travels behind someone or something."[5] Did you catch that? Someone or something. You can't follow well if you don't have someone or something to follow. You can't be a follower if you don't know who or what you follow. That is the basic principle of being a follower. It seems to be common sense.

If you can't identify one thing that drives all your decisions, then maybe you are a multi-follower. Do you change your mind from day to day based on what feels best to you at that moment? Then I'd say you are less of a follower and more of a narcissist. *Narcissism* is defined as "excessive interest in oneself," and this trait can make it difficult for individuals to acknowledge or pay attention to others. For a narcissist, the role of others is to provide praise, encouragement, support, and admiration to them.[6] Ouch. This sounds much like someone who would teeter around based on what stroked their ego in the moment. If you don't narrow your followship, you will continue to wander.

Typically, we see rebellions or mass movements initiated by a charismatic leader who has inspired thousands to take unconventional action. You may be easily swayed to follow stirring crowds based on who has the shiniest marketing or more immediate payout. The Bible warns us against this type of immaturity.

> "We will no longer be infants, tossed back and forth by the waves, and blown here and there by every wind of teaching and by the cunning and craftiness of people in their deceitful scheming" (Ephesians 4:14).

If you are going to follow, follow well. The Who or what to follow should be rather obvious if you are a believer. The answer is Jesus. To sit, watch, learn, and reflect on everything about Him is the wisest decision you could ever make. To follow anything else is a waste of time.

A level of devotion is expected when you consider yourself a follower. If the leader is reliable and marching toward a shared vision, the devotion shouldn't be wayward. In this case, following Jesus is a matter of life or death. And He is the most reliable leader Who has or will ever walk the planet. He wasn't born into a wealthy family. He didn't have the most likes and comments on Instagram. He was quite controversial, and it ruffled the feathers of the powers that be. Actually, it's the same today. Those who follow Jesus aren't the most popular; they are opposed, they are accused, and more often than we realize, they are murdered. Is this extreme followship worth it? It only makes sense in our human minds to commit to this level of devotion if we owe our life to someone: a life for a life. Jesus has saved our eternal lives, so we owe Him ours.

We see this dedication displayed on the battlefield. Personally, I've never been in war. I am not a military veteran. But I do have the highest respect for those who protect and defend us, sometimes even giving their lives so that we may have ours. Freedom is not a free gift; it is a sacrifice made by soldiers and their families. Those soldiers don't go on the battlefield questioning the orders of their leader. The leader says jump, and they say how high. They don't demand to see the entire battle plan. They only plot the next set of orders. They have complete trust in their leader, and if followship leads to their death, that is a risk they are willing to take. Their mission is to abide by their commitment and be a devout follower.

These soldiers are not just followers; they are leaders. I feel inspired by their courage and conviction to stand in harm's way to defend millions of people they do not know.

When you follow well, you become a better leader. Whether you lead a business, a team, a Bible study, or little ones running at your feet, you are a leader. If you are reading this, you are a leader. To be a better leader, you must first follow the Leader Who gave His all for you.

Learning to Follow - Nick

When I was a kid, I didn't feel the need to fit in with my peers. Even though I deeply cared what they thought, their approval didn't hold me hostage. You may read that and think, *Oh, you must be a natural leader.* But the reality is, I struggle with confidence more than you can imagine. I have never had the courage to dive head first into my dreams. There has always been a constant tension between who I am and who I want to be.

Back in the day, I thought graduating from high school would generate a variety of opportunities to lead. I had hoped for a part-time job at my church. Three years later, after being poured into by great mentors, I had that opportunity. My pastor and associate pastor took time to personally invest in me and help me learn what it means to be a leader. Jesus modeled this perfectly when He told the disciples that a student is never greater than the teacher. He has given us an example to follow and said, "the Son of Man did not come to be served, but to serve, and to give His life as a ransom for many" (Matthew 20:28). In other words, the best way to lead is to serve. And the best way to lead is to follow the best leaders, starting with Jesus. The challenge comes when our discernment on who to follow becomes skewed.

Having been a student pastor for years, a major challenge I face is helping students see the value of choosing their leaders wisely. I worry about this for my own kids too. We all want to be a leader worth following, but first we need to be a follower worth leading. The mentors in my life have been patient with me. They've helped me to recognize that I talk too much. They've helped me to see that I listen too little. They've graciously, and at times not so gently, let me know where I was failing miserably. A good leader knows when to be soft and when to be tough. A good follower knows how to receive both types of instruction.

Bad Leaders - Laura

The pretentious religious leaders in early AD tried to trick Jesus with word games. They would bait Him to contradict Himself with Scripture. When Jesus was asked the most important of God's laws, He summarized it in two commands: to love God and to love others (Mark 12:28-34). I like to think of His command this way:

To love God is a following action.

To love people is a leadership action.

The religious leaders had access to the early books of the Bible; they knew the covenant God had made with Abraham, and they knew the Ten Commandments. They read the laws of Leviticus and held others to those same steep standards. They went to the temple to make their sacrifices and created a theatrical scene when giving money to the church or the needy. Their actions looked legit on the outside, but Jesus didn't buy it. He knew better and it was time to reveal the hypocrisy.

When Jesus answered one religious leader's question about the most important commandment, something changed within him. He began to see the light. The conversation in Mark 12 flows like this,

"'Well said, teacher... [This] is more important than all burnt offerings and sacrifices.'

Realizing how much this man understood, Jesus said to him, 'You are not far from the kingdom of God'" (Mark 12:32b-34).

This religious leader started to see Jesus as more than just a competing influencer. The wisdom Jesus had was unprecedented. The entire Old Testament points to a coming Messiah, so this leader was marinating on the possibility that Jesus could be the real deal. Could it be possible the actual Messiah was standing in front of his eyes? Many in our generation are walking this line as well. They are leaders who are not willing to become followers. Whether it's their pride, their doubts, or their fears, it's a shame that so many men and women enter the doors of our churches and never experience the peace of being a true follower.

A canyon can easily exist between head knowledge and heart surrender. Wisdom and knowledge can be polar opposites. We must recognize there is no such thing as being an almost Christian. Much like there is no such thing as being kind of pregnant—you are or you are not. Then why did Jesus tell the religious leader that he was "not far from the kingdom of God"? After all, being "not far" is still the equivalent of being lost and dying. That he would agree with Jesus's answer about the greatest commandment was to be expected, but what was surprising was when he replied, "This is more important than to offer all the burnt offerings and sacrifices required in the law." I know I'm getting preachy on you, but this is important. Lean in.

As if a light bulb came on, this religious leader confessed that being religious was not all about sacrifices and offerings. He had not yet acknowledged that Jesus was the Messiah, but his wheels were turning. To cross the finish line and win a forever relationship with Jesus, he must abandon his own way and fully follow Jesus (even His radical teachings). To love God is to follow God. Mark doesn't tell us any more about this conversation, and we are left wondering if this religious leader became a follower. I hope he did. It's not our responsibility to "save" anyone. It's our responsibility to lead others to follow Jesus.

Leading Well - Laura

The second part of the greatest commandment is to love people. We must step up to that plate. Welcome to leadership. Welcome to loving fast. Since Jesus was already on a roll breaking the chains of legalism, He (being Jesus) was able to summarize the entire message of the greatest commandments in four words: love God, love people.

Today we live in a self-focused society. The same was true back then. Every generation is surrounded with messages that reinforce getting what we want, when we want it, and how we want it. It's not uncommon to see those of influence look out for their own interests first (even if it means lying, cheating, and stealing). Thankfully, we aren't studying the behavior or influence of worldly leadership. We are learning to follow Jesus and inevitably become better leaders.

Nick and I were both psychology minors in college. Studying human behavior apparently fascinates us. There is a war within each of us to act selfishly or altruistically. This war became more evident to me when I laid down my career ambitions to attend school every day with our oldest son, Leland. Once I recognized my son needed a 1:1 aide (and the school could not provide it), I stepped into momma bear mode. It seemed like a no-brainer. When I recognized the magnitude of my call as his mom, I embraced the true meaning of living for someone else. I had to be 100% focused on earning a PhD in Leland-ness. I laid down what felt like my entire life: my safety net, my social life, my career, and any neurotypical expectations. All of those former priorities no longer mattered. All that mattered was getting help for my son.

If you are a parent, I bet you'd do the same. Parenting is very self-sacrificing, yet we do it almost without a wince. Imagine wiring your life to offer that kind of love and attention to someone outside of your family. My hope is that I learn to "value others better than myself," as Paul teaches in Philippians.

"Do nothing out of selfish ambition or vain conceit. Rather, in humility value others above yourselves, not looking to your own interests but each of you to the interests of others" (Philippians 2:3-4).

I do not believe this type of love is easy or born into us as a normal social skill. I believe it must be learned. It takes intentional practice. And as per any developed habit, the more attention and consistency given to it, the more likely we are to rewire our brains to practice it. I want you and me to mimic Jesus so closely and so often that we wake up looking for ways "to motivate one another to acts of love and good works" (Hebrews 10:24, NLT).

When we are having a good day, I want us to love fast.

When we are having a bad day, I want us to love fast. I want it to be ingrained in our hearts. It will be a lifelong journey, and the more we practice loving people and following the Leader, the more obedient we are to the greatest commandment: love God and love people.

To love fast and live slow as a follower of Jesus is to abide by His greatest commandment: love God and love people.

CHAPTER TEN

Big Action

*"Diligent hands will rule, but laziness
ends in forced labor" (Proverbs 12:24).*

Nick and I have tackled some pretty massive work projects in our lifetime. Take this book for example: it's
been six years in the making. Until we buckled down and
decided to trust God with the big picture, it was just another
"yea, we should do that one day" kind of thing.

Having felt the repercussions of being a workaholic in
my past, I tend to grow weary when God asks me to take
big action. Living slow doesn't mean sit back and enjoy 24/7
calm. Living slow means you are living for Him and His plans
only—resting joyfully, taking in the moment, and using that
time to recharge for God's next instructions. There may be
hustle and bustle in the thick of God's work, but you will
experience peace in the middle of His will. When He gives
us instruction, we shouldn't dabble. Instead we should fully
immerse ourselves. We shouldn't wade in slowly; we should
dive off the cliff. It takes courage. It takes trust. And it takes
unquenchable passion.

Have you ever felt compassion or conviction towards a

specific cause? Have you ever welled with emotion as you witnessed social injustice or hurting orphans? Can you pinpoint a time in your life when you were unexplainably moved to action? Set your mind back to that moment. The passion you felt wasn't an accident. God designed you and knows what makes you tick. He knows your every high and low. He put each skill, talent, and quirk in you. If you feel compelled to serve your church, neighborhood, community, or country in a certain way, perhaps He is getting you ready to take big action.

Nothing beats the big action that Nehemiah took in the Old Testament. I'm an Old Testament nerd. If you like history, stick with me. If you hate history, stick with me. This is a big deal. This guy's entire life pivoted when he encountered a fellow Hebrew who explained the continuing devastation of Jerusalem after having been conquered 153 years prior. That conversation sparked a flame that ignited the reasons for our knowledge and admiration of Nehemiah today.

"When I heard these things, I sat down and wept. For some days I mourned and fasted and prayed before the God of heaven" (Nehemiah 1:4).

Nehemiah lived in Babylon and could have continued his career working with the king. Yet he could not quiet his anguish after hearing of Jerusalem's condition. He couldn't shake the compulsion to use his skills and energy to rebuild the wall around the city in order to restore Jerusalem's safety and dignity. Jerusalem was exposed and vulnerable. Having no walls to protect a city was like keeping a wound unbandaged and at risk for infection. This wound had been left unbandaged for 153 years as the city still lay in ruins. Why rebuild the walls now?

By this point, many Jewish people had moved away from Jerusalem to plant roots in their hometowns. The Hebrew people who had once lived in Jerusalem had scattered. Only the truly devoted were willing to return to their broken city, even in the dust of destruction. But God always has perfect timing, even when the big action He calls for doesn't seem to make sense. The big action He may ask of you may not make sense either.

Knowing the backdrop of the nation of Israel helps us understand the magnitude of Nehemiah's courage. If we want to be brave like him, we need to walk with him through this story. God chose to position Nehemiah at a place, in a position, and in a generation that would awaken his calling. He was already a well-respected man in the Persian government. Nehemiah served as the king's cupbearer.

Originally, the function of a cupbearer was to taste (either for quality or for poison or for both), carry, and serve wine to his master. In a case like that of Nehemiah, a cupbearer for royalty was not just a personal servant but also a trusted confidant and advisor. Thus, it was an office of great responsibility, power, and honor in the Persian Empire.[7]

Even at the peak of his career, Nehemiah was deeply troubled and willing to give up his entire life. He knew he could put his leadership and experience into that mission. It was certainly a major undertaking, and Nehemiah was afraid. Instead of letting fear win, he prayed. He prayed, then made a plan and took action. As the first order of business, Nehemiah had to request permission from the Persian king to travel to Jerusalem to rebuild the wall.

> "O Lord, please hear my prayer! Listen to the prayers of those of us who delight in honoring you. Please grant me success today by making the king favorable to me. Put it into his heart to be kind to me" (Nehemiah 1:11).

Those five words can turn any day around: *Please grant me success today.* Wow! Nehemiah, you're my favorite. And God did deliver the request of his bold prayer. But it wasn't that day. It was the following spring when the king gave him permission to leave for Jerusalem. In spite of the risk of approaching the king with a request like this, Nehemiah didn't stop.

When the request to leave his responsibilities and run to Jerusalem (a city conquered by the Persians) was granted, Nehemiah pressed further and asked for letters that would give him permission to pass through threatening cities. And there's more. This guy was relentless. He had a fire in his belly, leaving no stone unturned until his mission was complete. He went on to ask for the king to pay for it all. Seriously?

Now why would the king of an enemy country give Nehemiah access to strengthen a city he had proudly conquered, fund the mission himself, and then send his own army officers and horsemen to protect Nehemiah's entourage along the way? The only explanation is, "the gracious hand of God had been on [him]" (Nehemiah 2:18). When God sends you to accomplish a mission, don't be surprised if the impossible happens for you as well.

The first step must have been the hardest for Nehemiah, much like it is for you and me when we are timid to initiate a big action. Yet it was because of this first step that he had the courage to ask for constant help, and God granted his request. We must follow Nehemiah's example. Pray, plan, have courage, and take action.

Pride Comes before the Fall - Laura

Social media makes it easy to get the cart before the horse. Many times when we are excited about feeling God's affirmation in our lives, we spill all the beans publicly before we do any work behind the scenes. Our hearts and minds are eager to tell the world, and we spoil the dream by talking about it before we confirm that it's in the cards. We experience the endorphins of a job well done before we even lift a finger. I speak from personal experience. When an idea pops into my head, I want to run with it before any details are mapped out. More often than not, my big idea lasts a few weeks then fizzles because I'm overwhelmed by the hype I created and the lack of effort I put forth early on. I soon realize I had no bandwidth with which to execute the idea in the first place, but now everyone knows about it, and they will equally know the level of my failure. I climb the highest mountain to talk big about all of my dreams, and then they flop. When you are that high up, the fall hurts.

If you are passionate enough to tell the world about your dreams, make sure they are rooted and inspired by the ultimate Dream Giver. The Author and Perfector of our life holds the best plans for us in His hands. If we choose to take big action without Him, He may have to take our dream away from us in ways we didn't expect, resulting in some bruised egos.

Instead of telling God my big plans, I've learned (the hard way) to surrender first. It shouldn't be surprising that Nehemiah laid out this example when he chose to keep the "plans God put in his heart" (Nehemiah 2:11) to himself. What he did to channel his passion was to obtain some field experience. He scoped out the current condition of the wall of Jerusalem. He investigated how grim things really were. He got organized and made plans to present his vision to the leaders who would be able to help him accomplish this major construction.

Nehemiah did not bring just his passion to this monumental task; he brought years of experience as a planner, organizer, and motivator. He was a leader of leaders. He trusted that the Lord would go before him and prepare the hearts of the people who needed to team up to fulfill God's calling. This wall was not a one-man job. Men gathered the necessary resources and committed to build the portion of the wall in front of their own homes. Many goldsmiths and tradesmen took on more than their fair share because they became just as passionate as Nehemiah. They "worked enthusiastically" (Nehemiah 4:6) from "sunrise to sunset" (Nehemiah 4:21).

Loads of people rallied behind Nehemiah to pull their weight in this project but, per usual, faced opposition. You will face naysayers and critics too. These Israelites were ridiculed by neighboring kingdoms, yet they "continued the work with even greater determination" (Nehemiah 6:9). Can you believe it? These men were threatened and mocked, their resources were withheld and obstructed, yet they kept their eyes on their leader and kept the charge. These men were 100% committed. They never even removed their work clothes or armor. Day and night they were single-minded.

"None of us—not I, nor my relatives, nor my servants, not the guards who were with me—ever took off our clothes. We carried our weapons with us at all times, even when we went for water" (Nehemiah 4:23, NLT).

These men were in the zone. They trusted their leader, and they were following his example and vision to the point where they didn't even stop to bathe or break. The calling God had instilled in Nehemiah's heart was so evident that they gave up their comforts and safety. When we follow God's big dreams, our teams can morph into worker bees who work with us because it's a God movement.

Building the wall was a miracle. Through Nehemiah's relentless pursuit to complete his mission, this group of people completed the wall in 52 days. This type of project should have taken years. When God calls us to do something, He can accomplish far greater things than we could ever imagine. He likely already has His plan mapped out; He's just looking for someone to say yes. Nehemiah didn't set out to be important or beg God to make him famous. He simply listened to the conviction in his heart and got to work. God orchestrated this journey from start to finish. He chose to use Nehemiah as a vessel to complete His plan. I can get on board with that.

Getting to the Other Side - Nick

I am not a big dreamer. Perhaps I am afraid to dream big. Most of my life I've played it safe, and the most ambitious thing I've ever done was ask Laura to be my wife. Fast forward to our first year of marriage; we've bought a house and are living an unassuming life right outside of Atlanta. We didn't mind the unassuming life, but we were restless. I was in a rough place personally as I struggled to get through another day as a teacher. I felt God was moving me to take a step of faith into new territory, but I feared what people would think: my parents, Laura's parents, my mentors, and others, not to mention how my bosses would react to my telling them I wasn't coming back. Through a series of conversations and events, God gave us a peace that it was time to move on.

Crashing into a job search for ministry-related work, I welcomed a few potential opportunities that landed in my pipeline. Excited and hopeful, when it came time to renew my contract as a teacher, I went to my principal and told him my plans to move on. He was gracious but concerned. He told me he would give me until June to decide for sure, which was 2-3 months past the contract deadline. He knew I hadn't locked in another job and didn't want my newly married self to be jobless. Smart guy.

June came and I still didn't have a solid opportunity kicking down my door for a full-time job. If you are a teacher looking to get out of that profession, it is tough. You have such a small window to make that choice with certainty. Laura and I talked it over and came to the conclusion that God was asking us to take a leap of faith. My principal was shocked when I told him the news. It must have seemed crazy for someone to make a decision with nothing to fall back on. I was sweating it all the way to the end of August, which just so happened to be when I got my last paycheck as a teacher. That same month I was offered a full-time position at a church down the road. God provided seamlessly.

The hardest part of that big step of faith was fielding the

questions from family. Explaining and justifying our decision was a challenge because the overall answer was, "God has called us to something different. If it falls through, we will work it out. If it doesn't, you will all know God was in this the whole time." It was discouraging when those closest to me caused my faith to shake. *Was this really something God asked us to do? Or are we chasing rabbit trails? How can I be sure God is leading me to take this big action? If I fail, is that also a part of Your plan, Lord?* There is a fine line between walking in faith and walking in feelings. We prayed for wisdom, and He provided the strength to see our calling through.

Tackling a big goal means taking one bold step in the right direction. What feels like an insurmountable wall in front of you might look like a speed bump in your rearview mirror. I'm not going to promise that your choices will always pan out like ours did. I've had other leaps of faith that resulted in outcomes far outside what I had envisioned. Far outside! That's the hardest part actually. We all want a great story on the other side. We all want to be seen and heard and to inspire with our stories of faith and obedience. The truth is, most of our stories won't lead to heroism. If you are willing to pray, plan, and take action for the cause God has put in your heart, the outcome won't matter because you will know you are simply walking in obedience. It's not the destination that matters; it's the journey. God will turn you into who you were meant to be if you let Him.

To love fast and live slow with a big idea, be like Nehemiah. Pray, plan, have courage, and then take big action.

CHAPTER ELEVEN

Big Obedience

*"He looked down on the people of Israel
and knew it was time to act" (Exodus 2:25).*

I'm (Nick) not an introvert. I'm as extroverted as you can possibly imagine, but speaking in front of crowds was something that terrified me from a young age. Starting in high school, I was occasionally asked to play music or lead worship. The church I attended, as well as other churches, would ask me to help them out. It was cool. But I'm not a good singer at all. I've always had a passion to lead worship, but that doesn't fit if you don't have a solid singing voice. Even still, they asked, and although I was uncomfortable, I said yes. As long as I was holding a guitar, I could get through.

Later in college, I had to take a public speaking class. By this time, I had realized I was called to work in ministry. I had always felt that I would have the chance to speak to groups at some point, but I was terrified at the thought. Slowly but surely I found my voice. It wasn't long before I had the privilege of traveling and playing with a small worship band throughout the southeast and, ironically, was asked to speak at these same events. I wasn't out there looking for new gigs. Truth be told, I didn't know how to network my way in that direction anyway.

One summer I had traveled to Mississippi for a student missions trip. I knew no one from the church except the student pastor, and we had only had a few interactions. Our whole band did not go this time, which was unusual. It was just me and my cousin Evan. After getting situated, we thought the first night went well. We had a nice little set up with the two of us, and the student pastor communicated a great message to the students.

Later that first night as things were winding down, the student pastor received a call that his wife was in early labor and their first child was on the way. Surprise! Little did I know that I was their backup camp pastor. He asked if I was willing to take over for the next four nights. I was underqualified and overwhelmed. But God moved in those next four nights. It was as if, in all my insecurity, God reassured me of my future. After that weekend, I knew God was preparing me for my place in ministry. It takes big obedience to conquer fear. My battle with fear is still a daily occurrence, but I know that with each step forward, He is preparing me to be who I am meant to be.

Each of you is gifted uniquely. You may not see it; others may not see it yet. Make no mistake though, God has given all of His children gifts to serve others and make His kingdom greater. The most effective way to pinpoint how you can use your gifts is to look at where your passion and talents merge. What moves you? What puts excitement in your life and butterflies in your gut? Everything has to pass the Scripture test, but if your passion connects with the heart of God through

Scripture, find a way to turn that passion into serving others and building God's kingdom.

If you know Jesus, God has given you a gift, and the purpose of that gift is to serve and work for the common good of those around you, primarily for building up God's people. Paul tells us in 1 Corinthians 12:7, "Now to each one the manifestation of the Spirit is given for the common good." Sometimes you will be obedient and not see the results. Choose obedience again anyway.

Teachers See Your Potential - Laura

When I was in high school, I was selected to be a part of a leadership program for students who demonstrated above average skills in one of these categories; art, literature, mathematics, music, science, or social studies. It was a scholarship program. And on the outside, I was flattered and seemed to be a qualified candidate per my extracurricular résumé. But on the inside I was terrified and felt like a fraud. To assure you that I'm not coming across with false humility, I didn't win the scholarship. I didn't pass go. I didn't collect the $10,000. Because it felt so over my head, I nearly skipped the interview. These teachers obviously saw something in me that I didn't see in myself.

Teachers do that. My mom was a teacher. My sister was a teacher. Nick's aunt and uncle are teachers. It runs deep in our family. Good teachers have a special gift of being able to see their students from a birds-eye view. They see the potential that can blossom if it's nurtured. (Teachers, you are super heroes. Thank you for all you do.) Okay, back to the story. My teachers in high school apparently saw potential in me, and I hesitantly walked alongside them when they knew the time was right.

You know who else does that? Our ultimate Teacher. God did this same thing to a guy named Moses. He was selected to do something pretty major, and his first reaction was, "But who am I to do such a big thing?" When you read the first few chapters of Exodus, you can smell his insecurity from a mile away. I don't blame him. His entire life had been unconventional and full of critics mocking his every move.

Moses was the guy whose mom put him in a basket and sent him floating down the Nile River in order to save his life. At the time, the Pharaoh was trying to do some population control amongst the fertile Israelite nation. He was intimidated at how big and powerful the Israelites had become, and he flexed his leadership muscle as he ordered for all newborn Hebrew baby boys to be thrown into the river. It's true. How tragic.

Moses's mom was a rebel. I like her. She hid Moses for three months "until she could no longer keep him hidden" (Exodus 2:3, CEV) and then had to make the hardest decision of her life: To put her baby in the basket and have faith that whatever happened was in God's plan.

As a mom, that is insane strength. I have a hard enough time not helicoptering over my own children. Her love for her son and her faithfulness to the Father gave her supernatural strength to let go of her own desires and trust God with the outcome. Her decision changed the world.

"The daughter of Pharaoh came down to bathe at the Nile, with her maidens walking alongside the Nile; and she saw the basket among the reeds and sent her maid, and she brought it to her. When she opened it, she saw the child, and behold, the boy was crying. And she had pity on him and said, 'This is one of the Hebrews' children" (Exodus 2:5-6, NASB).

As if that weren't a miracle enough, his sister Miriam had followed the basket along the riverbank. When she saw the Egyptian princess retrieve her baby brother, she revealed herself and offered to find a Hebrew woman to nurse him. The princess, it seems without hesitation but almost with gratitude, accepted the suggestion and offered to pay a Hebrew woman to nurse the baby and return him to her when he was old enough.

Pause. I want to recap two main characters. First, we have Pharaoh, who held ultimate power in Egypt. He was a coward who feared that the Hebrew slaves would stir up a rebellion and, as a selfish defense, ordered genocide of the coming generation. Second, we have Moses's mom. She was faced with the unthinkable yet outsmarted those in charge.

I would have loved to be a fly on the wall when Pharaoh's daughter came prancing into the palace with a Hebrew boy in her arms. Pharaoh's own daughter ignored his order and grew fond of the people he despised. Way to rub it in, God.

The Right Ingredients - Laura

Moses grew up having quite the internal battle. He was a Hebrew by ethnicity, but he sat at the Pharaoh's table. The Egyptians despised the Hebrew slaves, and I am sure that toxic prejudice stung the ears and heart of Moses. Even if he felt conflicted, Moses still enjoyed the perks and pleasures of being royalty. He was able to come and go as he pleased, unlike his fellow Hebrew people who were brutally beaten, overworked, and underfed.

According to Pharaoh, Moses's destiny should have been at the bottom of the Nile River. Nonetheless, God was curating one of His own people to have the inside scoop of Egyptian culture and power. No one knew it at the time, but Moses would soon be combating the very powers that had raised him. He'd have to go against the hands that fed him and the home where he had laid his head for decades.

It wasn't long before Moses started seeing the harsh treatment of his people as unbearable. One thing led to another, and a scuffle left an Egyptian soldier dead and buried in the sand, courtesy of the warrior side of Moses. But his warrior side came too late because the Hebrew slaves had grown resentful toward Moses. I am sure they saw him as a traitor, one who tried to relate to them but rested comfortably and protected by his status in the palace. News of Moses's killing the soldier began to spread, and soon both the Egyptians and the Hebrews were against him. He certainly had a target on his back.

What did Moses do? He fled.

This is speculation, but perhaps Moses had not quite decided which side of the fence to plant his roots on and he ran to a nearby town called Midan. Fun fact: The Egyptian culture that Moses had grown up in was repulsed by the work of shepherds. It's humorous that God continued developing Moses by first humbling him. What do you think his new occupation was? You guessed it—a shepherd.

During that time in Midian as a shepherd, he developed a greater understanding and appreciation of the Hebrew culture, their work ethic, their values, and their unfaltering faith in the God of Abraham, Jacob, and Isaac. He married and named his first born son, Gershom, which means, "foreigner in a foreign land." The child was named in reference to Moses's past life as a prince of a people he did not belong to. He felt disoriented his whole life and understandably so.

God has a way of doing things. It's as if He were grabbing different ingredients from each stage of Moses's life, and when the recipe was complete, He called for this unlikely hero. Moses was rescued by his mother, raised by a princess, educated in Egypt, unwanted by his people, and now living a mundane life as a shepherd. It's not the ideal picture of a man of power. Throughout his life, God had been walking him through each season so he'd acquire the necessary skills to rescue and lead the entire nation of Israel.

Do you ever feel unqualified and insecure? I know we do. Isn't hiding in my bubble safer? There are born leaders, and then there are those like Moses. I can imagine he had a fair share of pity parties (or at least he had reason to, in my opinion). But for every notch in his metaphorical pity party belt, an ingredient was gained.

Because his mother gave him up, he was rescued.

Because he was raised in the palace, he was known by the most powerful.

Because he moved to Midian as a shepherd, he learned how to survive in the wilderness.

His was not the ideal storyline. God had to orchestrate all of these skills and strengths. No one could have predicted that Moses's life was the exact disaster recipe God needed to prepare the hero for Israel. And when Moses's Teacher told him it was his time to shine, he turned it down— twice. However, once all of these ingredients were in order, God said it was time, and you don't mess with God's plans.

Time to Act - Laura

I find myself asking God to answer prayers in my timing. I need, I want, I beg, and I plead. I sound like a needy daughter. Perhaps I am. He corrects me often. Yet no matter the fuss I make, He still works only at His own pace. His perfect pace. Patience is hard. We each have mud to plow through, bruised knees to toughen, egos to smash, and work ethics to sharpen. And when, and only when, God has pruned away the parts of our pride that could sabotage His plans, He decides it's time to act.

Can you imagine having been a Hebrew in Moses's time? Thanks to ol' Joseph's rescuing his family from the famine (which had occurred a few hundred years earlier), the family of Jacob, also known as Israel, moved to Egypt. About seventy-ish family members in total moved there and planted roots as shepherds. As humans tend to do, Joseph and his brothers grew old and passed away. By this point, the people of Israel had multiplied and very likely picked up some leadership roles in the country. Power, prestige, and wealth can stir up jealousy and tension. Soon enough, the native Egyptians grew hostile towards the burgeoning people of Israel. The new Pharaoh decided it would be in his best interest to rule over these foreigners.

Keep in mind that the nation of Israel had enjoyed freedom throughout their entire existence. Now due to their proximity to a power-hungry leader, they were forced to work as slaves, lay bricks, and build cities, monuments, and roads. Gone were the glory days. Things were about to get rough. The brutality continued to increase, and several generations later, the Israelites were still in captivity, all the while crying out to God and growing weary.

Can you imagine feeling this hopelessness for hundreds of years with no refuge? Even more so, can you imagine how they felt when Moses showed up as their knight in shining armor and their oppression became even more unbearable? Pharaoh cracked the whip (figuratively and literally), fuming with anger over Moses's demands. These people were desperate. They needed a hero, and no one believed Moses could fill those shoes.

If you are familiar with the story of Moses, you know that he continued to confront Pharaoh. God hardened Pharaoh's heart, and a whole slew of horrible (pretty cool, actually) plagues hit the country. Amazingly, the plagues skipped over the people of Israel. Eventually, God cursed Egypt by killing all the firstborn sons. At that moment the Pharaoh begged Moses to take his people and leave. The unlikely hero won the day. The cry of Israel was heard, and God won—in His timing as always.

Back to back we've learned about faithful men in the Bible who acted in obedience and accomplished something mighty. In the last chapter, you saw how Nehemiah had an impressive résumé and clear vision. He used his experience to rebuild Jerusalem's wall in 52 days. Moses, on the other hand, had many public failures and no solid life plan, yet he used his experience to rescue Israel from slavery. God can use anyone. It's not a matter of skill or talent; it's a matter of saying yes. God will only work at the speed of your obedience. Not a second before, not a second after.

To love fast and live slow is to obey Him even if you feel unqualified.

CHAPTER TWELVE

Big Mouth

"Do not let any unwholesome talk come out of your mouths, but only what is helpful for building others up according to their needs, that it may benefit those who listen" (Ephesians 4:29).

I (Laura) am not naturally a fiery person. Nick, on the other hand, would love more than anything to be given the task of punishing all the bad guys on the planet. I've never met anyone who wants to be a real life Avenger more in my life. Good thing God hasn't tasked him with that responsibility thus far because I'd never hear the end of it. I've never wanted to be an Avenger, but I do have a few things that ignite my fire for justice. One of those things is gossip.

By no means am I claiming not to have fallen into the trap of running my mouth, but it's a pet peeve to say the least. Judgment, criticism, and passive-aggressive jokes are all gossip's ugly cousins. If you are not leading with love, you are leading with selfishness. If you are not looking at people through a lens of love, you are looking at them through a lens of cynicism. If your coffee talk conversations revolve around life updates on people who are not present, you are walking a fine line. Your daily endorphins shouldn't come from discussing the latest scoop from your inner circles. Living for the juicy update is not living for Jesus.

Most of us can recall a time in our childhood when we were wounded by gossip. Perhaps you can recall several. We all have those stories. Personally, I can recall many times when I was the acting antagonist. I was acting one way on the outside and living another on the inside. Lies, criticism, and hate that overflow into the world are damaging. I know firsthand.

Mean Girl - Laura

This is not a proud memory. It brings me to tears just reliving the pain I caused during my short-lived mean girl stage. Short-lived but almost fatal. As a middle schooler, I desperately wanted to be cool. When you reach that age, peers are your biggest influencer, and my greatest desire was to belong.

During this already vulnerable time, my dad was actually fighting for his life with a rare form of leukemia. My parents went to the hospital every two weeks for his chemotherapy treatment to improve his chances of survival. The kids (three of us) were handed off to stay with friends or church families for weeks at a time until they were home and Dad was stable. For those who have gone through or watched a loved one endure the risky side effects of chemotherapy, you know it wipes out your entire immune system. And having three kids bringing school germs around just wasn't an ideal situation. Our family got used to the nomad life. All five of us have a different imprint from this time.

I fell hard and heavy into the warmth and acceptance of my church youth group. My sister wasn't as lucky. She was walking through an equally troubled time, and some of the girls in the youth group responded with rejection and gossip. It was deep, it was cruel, and it pushed her away. I watched this unfold right in front of my eyes. I didn't think I could stop it because who'd listen to me anyway? If I stood up to these older girls, how would that bring justice? I had no voice.

Fast forward to my seventh grade year. My cowardly silence toward those who had bullied my sister morphed into my cowardly acceptance of the same sin I had despised in them. Because I didn't stand up to the mean girls, I eventually became one. And this time, the arrows didn't push someone away from our church youth group; they almost took someone's life. Long story short, I teamed up with a few other mean girls and wrote a younger girl a nasty note. This was before social media days. You actually had to write with pen and paper to bash someone. It took a bit more effort, but the sting hurt in the same way. I can't even recall what the younger girl did to "deserve" hate mail. Perhaps it was a certain outfit she wore that we didn't like. Perhaps she looked at one of us the wrong way. Perhaps she really did do something hateful, but even if she did, she didn't deserve being bullied.

I was chosen as the messenger. We gathered all of our mean notes together into some fancy origami 1990s magic, and I passed it along. Never saying a word. No eye contact. Just a business transaction between my tribe of many to her tribe of one. That was it on my end. It seemed that the deed was done and over with. I passed the cool kids' initiation and was considered one of them. I'm not sure if I went home that day feeling like I had won, as if I had hit a popularity milestone, but the celebration was short lived.

That next week we found out that this young girl had attempted suicide. Here I was trying to elevate my life, and she was trying to end hers because of mine. I have never been more ashamed. There was no investigation or school-wide meeting to address bullying, but I knew I was at fault. This girl had already been through a lifetime of hurt behind the scenes, and I gave her the ammo to end it all.

There is power in our words. In a season where my dad was fighting for his life in the hospital and couldn't speak, I put a girl in the hospital by speaking hatefully. This changed me. Forever.

"The tongue has the power of life and death, and those who love it will eat its fruit" (Proverbs 18:21).

Speak Kindness - Laura

You'd be wrong to think this type of drama only happens in tween life. Nick and I have been the victims of gossip and rumors in our adult life, some of which resulted in a church small group rotting from the inside out. Many were ostracized because a rumor was never addressed or resolved. We found out weeks later about the slander and how it had poisoned many close friendships without the knowledge that our names were in the rotation. It's a shame. The Bible says, "Whoever goes about slandering reveals secrets; therefore, do not associate with a simple babbler" (Proverbs 20:19, ESV).

Not everyone thinks this way though. I can count on my fingers, toes, and likely Nick's as well how many times I've felt judged or shamed by adjacent parents. Parenting is a funny thing. Nick and I are learning the emotional patterns of each of our kids. We know what tricks they play and what discipline works best with their unique personalities. We call our oldest son "Demo," not because of the demolition he causes (although that applies 10x) but because he is our first attempt at this parenting thing. He is our demo. I dare to say I've learned more in the past seven years than I've learned in a lifetime. Raising a family has given us direction, purpose, and gray hair.

You think you will be the best parent on the planet until you become one. Smug internal monologues will come back to haunt you: *Hmm, did you see that tantrum? I would never let my kid act like that* or *Lighten up; a little extra fun and late bedtimes won't hurt.* During a grocery store meltdown (not from me if you were wondering), one helpful lady said, "Just give him the candy bar for breakfast; it won't kill him." She must not have had kids. Surely if she did, she would know from Parenting 101 that you don't let the tantrum win. And on that particular day, I was determined to be a winner.

I'll never forget the day I realized my parenting style was up for judgment. Our oldest was three years old. There is a 100% chance I had already made four million parenting mistakes by this point, but we were finally getting into the swing of things. This child is our free spirit. Such a spirit is both delightful and exhausting, which only meant that the much anticipated year-end preschool musical was sure to be entertaining. Get a bunch of three-year olds on stage with maracas, and let the iPhone videos begin.

Every stereotypical behavior you'd assume from a hyperactive toddler boy occurred during those seven minutes on stage—except ripping his clothes off and streaking, which has happened in many public places but not on this particular day. Rounding the end of their second song, he spotted me in the audience recording him. We exchanged waves. You know the feeling—when you hope everyone notices his adorableness and you sheepishly giggle because, although you are visualizing him receiving a gold medal for charm, you want to remain humble.

Not five seconds later, he proceeded to interrupt my daydream by shouting, "Mommy, put the phone down!" motioning for me to cut it out, as if I were embarrassing him. I laughed it off and put my phone away, not to distract his Tony-winning performance. In my ignorance, I did not notice the gasps of surprise coming from the moms around me. After the kids bowed, my wild child had to be assisted off the stage because he wouldn't leave the microphones alone. A mom came up to me,

"You sure have your hands full."

"Yes, he certainly keeps us on our toes."

"I can't believe you let him talk to you that way."

"What do you mean?"

"You can't let him tell you what to do. Nip that now before it gets worse."

In complete shock, I didn't know whether I wanted to crumble or snap back. From a place of pride, I wanted no mom giving me unsolicited parenting advice. I was dumbfounded that she had felt compelled to walk across the auditorium to tell me anything other than, "Our kids are adorable, aren't they?" I wanted to shame her. Yet when I slowed down and reflected on my judgment toward others, I realized I do the same thing. Really, we all do.

I am quick to criticize and justify my judgments because I need some sort of validation of my deepest insecurities. We tend to point out faults based on our own flaws. This mom must have been through a hard time with her child recently. Maybe she had been criticized or shamed as well. Looking over the fence and judging a neighbor's parenting style places you in opposition to God. Having a critical spirit steals our joy and peace, making it impossible to delight in the differences amongst us.

The Bible is full of Scripture about gossip and slander, as well as kindness. I want to share these verses with you to extinguish the flames of any critical hearts:

- Don't judge anyone by your human limitations. Only God's judgments are flawless (John 8:15-16).

- Don't be quick to condemn someone else's actions. God is patient, but He doesn't overlook anyone's disobedience (Romans 2:1-5).

- Don't attack each other. Try to be a good example so others won't copy your bad behavior (Romans 14:13).

- Don't speak destructive things about others. Are you qualified to perfectly judge someone else (James 4:11-12)?

Loving Everyone - Nick

Gossip, slander and hatred towards another can manifest in many ways. If your identity is one of crushing accusations, against yourself or others, or the exclusion of others based on the choices they make, the color of their skin, or the countries they come from, your identity is not in Jesus. We plead with others to know Jesus; we want lives to be changed. But we cannot draw lines in the sand about the ones we are willing to love and share Jesus with.

You may not know whom you want to marry. You may not know what you want to be when you grow up. Heck, I don't know what I want to be when I grow up. But my worth is not found in what I do. My worth is in Whom I belong to. I know that may sound cliché, but that's okay. I'll take cliché. You be you, and I'll be me. And if we trust in Jesus and the image He's given us, we can be confident in how He made us. That's where my self-worth comes from, and I hope yours does too.

I have this idea—no, a vision—of what the mission to love fast and live slow could look like if a mass of people bought into the concept. I see people realizing the gifts they have. I see people using those gifts the way God intended for them to be used, and then I see unbelievers seeing Jesus and choosing to follow Him.

Heart breaking—that's what comes to mind when I see the way much of the church has responded and reacted to the political climate we are currently facing. If you think that blasting the side you disagree with is going to change someone's view, you are wrong. Blasting other's views and values will never open doors to talk about real issues. If you want to be effective and make a difference, start building meaningful friendships with people who hold opposing views. Learn who they are and love them for the fact that they are created in God's image. There has been too much of the opposite behavior for a long time; it has become the accepted norm. Accepted norm, however, is rarely the same as God's way.

James is very clear that the tongue is our most powerful tool for both good and bad. He compares the ability of a small spark to cause a massive forest fire to the potential for our big mouths to cause that kind of destruction in the lives of others if we are not careful (James 3:5). We must become more intentional in the use of our big mouths as a means of encouragement and love instead of tearing down those who don't share our same views or opinions.

To love fast and live slow is to avoid gossip or slander and find ways to lift one another up.

CHAPTER THIRTEEN

It's Okay to Be Different

"Before I formed you in the womb I knew you,
before you were born I set you apart"
(Jeremiah 1:5).

I (Nick) always found it funny when my friends that were seemingly passionate about being unique were actually trying to fit in with the other "unique" kids. The kids that were bent on being different were focused on being noticed and on trying to start a fresh trend of "differentness," if that's even a word. Being different became the norm. It was a strange anomaly, for sure. As I said a few chapters back, I was semi-okay with who I was when I was younger. I walked around my college campus wearing my torn-up jeans, Captain America tee shirt (before comic heroes were cool again), and my red, white, and blue Converse Chuck Taylor's. I had no distinct style of my own on a day-to-day basis and was totally okay with that.

It wasn't until I got older that my confidence became shaky and my identity was uncertain. Rewinding to the turning point, it started when I was let go from a job at a church back in 2013. No single event in my life has made me feel more like a failure than being fired by a guy who was at one point my closest friend. What hurt the most though is that I wanted to fit into the mold the church needed, but I didn't. I couldn't. It wasn't in me; I could tell from the moment I walked in the doors of my office on my first day. You always hope that the weary feeling is simply first-day blues, but now I know it was discernment. If I realized all of this, why did I stick around? Why did I do everything in my power to fit in? I wanted to belong. I didn't want to be different. Even though I didn't want to be there, I wanted to be accepted.

We all want to belong. We all want to bring something good to the table and feel valued. We all long for community. My situation had multiple problems. First, I tried to force my spot on the field. I was a square peg in a round hole. My colleagues were the kids with the wooden hammer trying to squeeze me into a hole where I was never going to fit. My personality and philosophy were different. It's okay not to fit in everywhere. We can become so distracted with trying to fit in that we rarely stop to evaluate if we are even meant to be in that particular spot. I made that mistake for about a year and suffered because of it.

Second, I had moved my family from Florida to Georgia for this job. Of course, I just didn't know how to admit that it wasn't working out. My solution was to change who I was and become who they needed me to be. That is a toxic recipe for any employee-employer relationship. I failed miserably. They saw it and I saw it. I kept telling myself that it would get better. I held out hope that there would be another position created where I could thrive.

The third reason I wanted to fit in was that the church

and its leaders were cool. They were! They were the most forward-thinking church around. The church was growing rapidly, and I was getting to meet and rub shoulders with influencers I admired. With all of these great perks, I wanted to become whoever I needed to be if it meant I could stay. It rarely works out that way.

You need to know that you will not fit in everywhere you go. It's okay to be different. Embrace who you are in Christ and trust Him with your identity. I went through a couple of years of anxiety and battled depression after I was let go. Being fired stinks. But thinking that you were fired because you weren't cool enough and couldn't fit in is even worse. I had to get to a point where I embraced who I am and who God has gifted me to be.

God doesn't make mistakes. If you are in a place right now where you are trying to keep your head above water but you can't quite figure out why, maybe you're a square peg like I was. Actually, maybe we are stars...that's it, a star peg trying to fit in a square hole. Be a star. If there is no star-shaped hole, you're probably in the wrong galaxy. Embrace who you are and be you.

No Fiesta - Laura
Our oldest son, Leland, had quite the roller coaster experience in kindergarten. As a result, this Momma did too. We knew our Leland wasn't going to fit in a box. And quite frankly, mainstream classrooms are more for kids who play nicely in that box. That's not a bad thing at all—just not the right fit for our Leland.

It's always beneficial to give background details in order for the overall scenario to make sense. Backing up to when he was completing his pre-kindergarten year, Nick and I were left trying to decide which school would be the best fit for his learning style. After much prayer, we decided to withdraw him from his current public school and enroll him in a new private Christian school down the road. We knew the staff and explained the developmental delays we felt made him stand out. We didn't want anything to be a surprise. They accepted our application, and by the skin of his teeth, Leland passed their interview process. The situation at the new school seemed like it was going to fit like a glove. By fit like a glove I mean, everything would work out fine as long as Leland changed the way he learned and self-regulated, as long as he didn't act out, as long as he didn't make a scene, as long as he acted normal, and as long as he looked neurotypical.

It only took 3.5 seconds to identify how different he was from his peers. The first day of kindergarten will forever go down as one of my most painful days as a parent. It wasn't just the meltdowns, the running, the hitting, the yelling, the panic, or the emergency parent-teacher meeting in the principals office. It was the humble awakening that a lot more was going on under the surface of my strong-willed little boy. Things began to escalate until there was no more denying that his Leland-ness (coined by his neuropsychologist) was over our heads.

Later that semester his school had planned a class fiesta to celebrate their first quarter of school. They invited all of the parents to come watch the kids sing songs and show off their artwork—you know, a major milestone and moment of pride for a sweet kindergartener. This event was on the decorated calendar that was viewed every morning. They even had a daily countdown to this Friday fiesta. Leland would come home each day and tell us, "Eight more days until the fiesta!" or "Five more days, Mom!" or "Mommy, Daddy, it's tomorrow! or "The fiesta is tomorrow!" We were overjoyed to see him look forward to school that week.

The big day came. I had big plans. To surprise Leland, I was going to bring along his little brother and sister so they could look upon their big brother's greatness. I rehearsed their cheers, "That's my big brother! He is so cool." I knew Leland would beam with excitement. One o'clock rolled around, and I had my two littlest ones buckled in and cruising down the road to the school. We didn't want to miss a second of watching Leland shine. He deserved it. We deserved it. Our family felt pretty worn down from the constant struggle we felt with school each day. After all of those months of trying new strategies and constant sensory breaks, we craved one positive afternoon.

Then it happened. The phone call. It was 1:30 p.m. and the fiesta started at 2:00 p.m.

"Hi, Laura?"

"Hi, this is Laura. Everything okay?"

"Yes, Leland is okay! But he's had a rough day, and we gave him three chances to straighten up. Unfortunately, he lost his chances. He will not be able to join us for the fiesta this afternoon. Will you be able to pick him up?"

My heart dropped. Is this real life? Had they told him? What happened? A war of emotions stirred inside me. Although he had not yet been diagnosed on the autism spectrum, I knew he processed things differently and what could come across as disobedient might very well be accidental. I knew his sensory needs would be high that day because he was excited and anxious. When he is heightened, it becomes nearly impossible for him to regulate his hyperactivity and impulsivity. I was broken over this news.

When I arrived at the school, I pulled up to the front door. The principal greeted me with a grim, almost apologetic look on his face. He offered to stand by the car with the other little ones while I went inside to capture Leland. Walking through the double doors, I heard Leland crying. Mind you, this was a very small school: one classroom with eight students. They were renting a wing of a church for their classroom and cafeteria area. To hear your son crying from down the hall meant the entire staff and all of his classmates heard him too. Without saying a word, without reprimanding, without shaming him even more, I scooped up my 60 lb whimpering son and carried him out of those double doors. I will never forget that cry.

I am sure Leland will have many more heartbreaks during his life. Since I am a mom who truly loves her son and wants to see him grow and develop, I am not afraid to see him walk through hard times. Hard times develop character. But the weeping from his heart that day was rooted in misunderstanding. He didn't understand what he did to be uninvited.

As Leland's arms bear hugged my neck and he wrapped his legs around me, he kept crying, "Why can't I go to the fiesta? I want to go! I am so sorry!" I wanted to crumble at that moment. I am crumbling now reliving it. Not because I am resentful or angry that the school enforced its rules and structure. We support that. We encourage that. After the fact, the staff and I recognized that it was all a misunderstanding. Leland was heightened and needed to self-regulate with a sensory break. He is what you call a sensory seeker. He needs pressure and impact to awaken his nervous system to get in the right gear. To a six-year-old trying to self-regulate, that day it looked like jamming a pencil in the pencil sharpener after being asked to stop three times.

If you are a parent of a neurotypical child, you may not understand, not because you don't care but because it's hard to know what you don't know. When you are raising an atypical child, you can throw out the parenting books. This pencil-jamming incident was not a moment to shed consequences, but no one knew it at the time. As I held him tight and carried him to my car, I knew he wanted to feel safe. We'd go over the sequence of events later, but in that tender moment, he needed grace and compassion. So we hugged and we cried.

Rite of Passage - Laura

Perhaps Leland had seen that day as a rite of passage. Perhaps he just wanted to be normal and accepted. To stand shoulder to shoulder with his classmates and present a song to all the families may have been his proclamation to the world, a proclamation that he'd accomplished a quarter of kindergarten even if it was 4x harder than for anyone else. But what Leland didn't know is that God had big plans for him, even if his fiesta looked different than what he expected.

When we got home, I scoured the kitchen, ordered some party supplies, and threw together an impromptu fiesta at our house for dinner. We wore hats. We ate too much guacamole. We even had a piñata and laughed until we cried. The next day we surprised the kids with a day trip to Disney World (#annualpassholders). We decided to use this fiesta fiasco as a teaching moment for the entire family. We had to rewire our brains from expecting normal and allow God to map out a new path.

Oftentimes we fixate on our own plans, our own mani-fested rite of passage, and we won't stop until we get there. If what we visualized doesn't come to fruition as a result of a few bumps in the road, the heartbreak is deep. But what if God had a different (and even better) experience planned for you this whole time? What if what you were hoping for is subpar to the gift God has behind His back? It is easy to be misunderstood; unfortunately, not every time is it our fault. And not every time will we get what we were hoping for. To love fast and live slow, we must surrender that heartache to God and keep a good attitude on the journey.

"If you, then, though you are evil, know how to give good gifts to your children, how much more will your Father in heaven give good gifts to those who ask him!" (Matthew 7:11).

What We Want Versus What God Gives Us - Laura
Since God made us all different, we should embrace diversity with compassion and empathy. I cannot count on my fingers the number of times we've walked through a public place and one of the kids said assertively, "That's just how God made him, right?" We've seen amputees, we've seen facial deformities, we've seen eye patches, we've seen cancer pa-tients, we've heard and seen Tourette tics, and we've heard mumbling and stuttering. Kids stare. And their immediate response has become, "Mom, God makes everyone diffe-rent, and that's okay." It's a proud mom moment. I won't lie.

A hard question to answer though is, "Mom, why did God make them that way?" I don't always have the answer. I do not know God's every intention or strategy. But I do believe that He loves us and makes no mistakes: even the sweet babies lost before taking their first breath and even those sweet children born with a disability deemed impossible to overcome. There is a very tender spot in my heart reserved for children who are misunderstood. They need love, acceptance, compassion, and a chance at their best life.

Earlier this month, I came across the story in Luke where Jesus healed a crippled man. His friends lowered him through a roof while Jesus was speaking to a crowd. The friends were eager to present their disabled friend to Jesus because they had heard about a previous miraculous healing. Getting Jesus to fix the external problem was on their agenda. To them, that was the most obvious setback.

Yet the first words out of Jesus's mouth were, "Your sins are forgiven" (Luke 5:20). Jesus did not see a broken man in front of Him. He saw a lost man in need of a Savior. That is the same condition we all come to Jesus with. We are all sinners in need of ultimate healing. We can come to Him with our list of wants, but Jesus fulfills our needs.

You may have prayed for healing, you may have been praying for restoration, you may have been begging God to save your marriage, but remember this: what Jesus cares about first and foremost is the condition of your heart. He looks past your appearance, your imperfections, and your disabilities and sees a child He created to bring glory to Him. That is the ultimate goal.

If you've been striving for affirmation from others and would do anything to feel accepted, be cautious. We weren't created to belong to this world. It is okay to feel homesick on this side of heaven. If you've ever been misunderstood or are raising someone who is, God's intention isn't to make your life harder; it's to develop your character. Give Him control and surrender your expectations. Do you really want to be ordinary? Isn't that so last year? Or are you willing to let God make you extraordinary? Don't be limited to your finite mind.

To love fast and live slow as you live outside the box, accept how God created you and delight in His creativity.

CHAPTER FOURTEEN

It's Okay to Slow Down

"Teach us to number our days carefully so that
we may develop wisdom in our hearts" (Psalm 90:12, CSB).

I (Laura) wish you could see my view right now. Looking right past my laptop, I see the bold horizon welcoming the sun to set along the waves. We are spending the week at the beach, one of my favorite (and easiest) spots to rest and recharge. Oh, did I mention we are at an all-inclusive resort? The kids are having a blast with the grandparents back home, and we are skipping through the week in pure stress-less bliss. Isn't living slow easy?

Okay, that paragraph is a complete lie. We are not at the beach. I am not gazing at the horizon. The view from my laptop is actually a never-ending pile of laundry, to-do lists that compound by the minute, an electric bill that is $75 higher than last month, and children rummaging through the pantry like mice looking for dinner. Isn't living slow hard?

It's undisputed that rest is good, yet our culture has found itself leaving no room for this vital behavior. The faster we get to our destination, the better—even at the cost of our mental and physical health. Thankfully I had a mom who knew better.

When your mom speaks, you should listen. Sure, there were (many) times when my teenage-self thought I was wiser than she, but the older I get, the more admiration I hold for her. My mom tends to redirect with gentle nudges. I'd roll my eyes each time she'd recite this warning: "Laura, you need to rest."

On more than one occasion, I remember thinking, *Mom, I'll sleep when I'm dead. I have to do this.* I have to do this? According to whom? Who told me I had to take on loads of projects, say yes to every request, be the top of my class, outdo my co-workers, stay up late to finish that degree, wake up early to exercise? Who said I had to do it all? According to my actions, my self-worth was wrapped up in how full I could pack my schedule. The busier I became, the more I could humble-brag about my accomplishments.

When I worked in corporate America, I burned the candle at both ends. Nick and I were newlyweds, and we'd fight over how late I'd stay at work. I missed our first wedding anniversary because my boss sent me on a work trip that had promise of a bonus upon return. This kind of compromise continued for years. It was a great company with great people, but when you put a recovering workaholic gal like me on the field, I will take it too far. Soon enough, after extending myself year after year, my body started to fight against me. I developed heart palpitations, adult acne, migraines, and even a scare with an oncologist because blood work came back wonky. There was a stretch of time when I traveled for 37 days in a row, not once putting my head on my own pillow. With all the airport travel, my immune system crashed, and I even caught swine flu when it was an epidemic in 2009.

Here I was running Laura's energy bank ragged, making all kinds of mistakes in the process because I was convinced that finished was better than perfect. I'd hear my Mom's voice, "Laura, you need to rest," and I'd resist out of fear of letting people down. After all, if I rest, how will the world keep turning? My work got sloppy. My boss even hit "reply all" one day to the team with a message that basically said, "Get it together, Laura." I knew this wasn't the quality work I had promised to deliver. I knew I was disappointing my company, team, and God. Thankfully our God is grace-filled. He is full of compassion and course corrections.

God taught me the power of living slow at the perfect time. We were in our first year of parenthood and still experiencing zero margin in our personal and work lives. Nick and I would walk the neighborhood, stroller in tow, and discuss the hope we held on to that one day we'd have more margin: white space on the calendar and cushion between the lines of to-do lists. We needed to recharge and refresh. We were certainly operating from empty cups.

One night, Easter Sunday 2013 to be exact, the phrase *love fast live slow* fell on my heart. I suppose that sounds super mystical. God and I don't have a direct line of communication, but I can oftentimes discern what comes straight from God. And this message was directly from the One above. Right after my conversation with Nick about creating margin in our lives, I began asking God how we could make this a reality. As new parents, both working full-time outside the home, how could we find time to grow personally and professionally and still have time for each other? It's the great mystery of the world.

I was up late that night. Maybe I was restless, or maybe the baby wasn't sleeping. But I journaled and prayed. It was as if I had a code in my mind I had to hack. I knew God wanted us to feel peace and live with purpose. I knew there was something greater than punching the clock each day. What significance could we hold onto as we plowed through these tiring days? What driving force could keep our engines turning? The answer I was given…just love fast and live slow.

I didn't wake up the next morning with an immediate change of heart or retrained mind. No, on the contrary I felt acutely aware of all of my shortcomings when it came to displaying love through my words and attitude. I didn't naturally wake up with a willing spirit. If anything, I'd wake up grumbling because I was holding Nick to the standard of whatever God was trying to teach me. If I was supposed to start loving fast and living slow, that meant Nick was supposed to be doing it too. Every time I saw Nick fall short of my personal convictions, I'd call him out. You know, like a really good wife who doesn't nag at all. Now that I knew God wanted me to live this way, I felt inspired but disgustingly far from that standard. As we've described throughout this book, this concept is a lifelong journey.

Boundaries - Nick

When Laura mentioned her new life mantra, we were out running errands. She sat in the passenger seat with her journal resting oddly on her lap. She finally broke her silence and resurfaced our previous conversation about feeling worn down. She said she wanted to run some ideas by me to see if they made sense. One thing you should know about Laura is that she often double checks to see if her ideas make sense to others. Her brain is constantly working. She says she is introspective; I'd agree and add on that she's overanalyzing.

She asked what I thought about when I heard the words *love fast live slow*. When I first heard the phrase, I thought it sounded cool. I, too, was burning the candle at both ends, so it sounded like something I needed to apply to my life. At first our application of this phrase was very different. For me, the live slow part meant more time at the lake or the beach. It meant enjoying things like sports and making hobbies more of a priority. In my mind, running from the things that were overwhelming me was living slow, but now I realize that this wasn't living slow at all. To avoid addressing the things that add stress to our life doesn't solve the problem. It took some time to apply this live slow concept to the areas where we had issues: our marriage, work, family, and finances.

I joined Laura in her introspective journey and began thinking more about what this concept meant to me. How could I adopt this love fast live slow thinking? I felt that in order to set aside time to do this, I would need to create boundaries. You can't do this by accident; you must set the stage and then let it happen.

In order to create healthy margin in our lives, we must be intentional. When our time is already slim and overextended, things can already be on the verge of conflict. I tend to make the mistake of needing to be busy. I want to be on the move and going, going, going. I don't like to sit at home and be inside very often. Laura, on the other hand, loves staying at home. She loves quiet and slow. She is fine to have no plans for days. This drives me nuts (understatement).

Our time is valued in very different ways. However, one thing we both love is creating memories as a family. One of our favorite things to do is spontaneously pack up our bags and stay in Orlando for a few nights. Disney World is the best, isn't it? You either love it or hate it. And we love it. We live slow by the pool or at one of the Disney parks. We have zero agenda or time constraints.

Obviously, that is not an everyday reality. It's a special occasion, and it's easier to live slow when you go away for a bit. What happens when you and your family are maxed out with no margin to create those live slow moments? You need to create boundaries: boundaries between you and your spouse, between you and your work, and between you and your kids. If you want more time to recharge your batteries, you must pencil it in.

How does that look for you? How are we supposed to pencil in time to recharge if our calendar has no white space? Well, for starters you have to learn to say no. Even to good things. Even to things you love and that have great value. A moment of truth for me is that I am literally struggling in this area right now. I have many responsibilities fighting for my time, and I'm having a tough time discerning what is most important versus what can wait or what someone else can do instead of me. That is the question you have to answer for yourself. What can wait? What can someone else do? If you really go over your schedule with a fine tooth comb, you'd find places to move around. You need it, your family needs it, the business you run and the people you work for need it. Everyone you interact with will benefit from your creating that margin.

Kopophobia - Laura

Kopophobia is defined as "the fear of becoming fatigued or exhausted, either mentally or physically. Feeling as though you are hanging on by a thread." This is a new word for me but not a new phobia. The older I get, the more rigid I become in my routine and daily schedule. Knowing the physical, mental, and relational damage that overworking can construct, my pendulum began to swing in the far opposite direction. I fear adding any new responsibility to my plate because feeling stressed out sucks. Can I get an amen? But what happens if you have no say regarding the responsibilities knocking at your door? How do you tackle them all? Is it possible to live slow while walking through a fast-paced season? The answer is yes.

In the poetic chapter at the end of Proverbs, adverbs such as *extends, stretches,* and *grasps* describe the actions of a noble woman.

"She stretches out her hands to the distaff,
And her hands grasp the spindle.
She extends her hand to the poor,
And she stretches out her hands to the needy"
(Proverbs 31:19-20, NASB).

Men reading this: don't think you can get out of this that easy. God expects you to hustle and get your hands dirty too. When I feel the world is weighing on my shoulders, I easily resort to panic or withdrawal.

From the Scripture above, we read "she" but these are qualities that can serve us all. We read that she pushes herself to new limits to finish a project. Do you ever do that? Do you doubt what you are capable of until you cross the finish line and celebrate your new milestone? It feels good to put in the hard work and reap what you sow. When I decided to follow Jesus, I didn't know He'd ask me to extend myself beyond comfort. I didn't know He would ask me to stretch farther past my limitations than I ever thought possible. No one told me He'd require me to grasp His Word for survival in this demanding world.

Now that I know, I have two choices: stress or surrender. I've chosen each of the possibilities on occasion, and from personal experience, the surrendering option reaps more benefit. An unexplainable peace overtakes me when I fully give God my plans, worries, ambitions, and insecurities. It's like I no longer have to strive or hold my breath for an outcome. I know that if I am living slow and fully surrendered to His path, all things will work out. Try it for yourself.

To love fast and live slow is to surrender the urge to be all and do all. Take a deep, slow breath and follow God's lead and pace.

CHAPTER FIFTEEN

It's Okay Not to Be Okay

"For the Spirit God gave us does not make us timid, but gives us power, love and self-discipline" (2 Timothy 1:7).

Men seem to have the hardest time not being okay. I (Nick) tend to be an expert at hiding the things I want unseen when I feel like I can't be open about my real feelings. I have already acknowledged that I'm an open book and wear my emotions on my sleeve. But oftentimes the emotions on my sleeve are not the really raw ones. Much of the emotion that I let out is a guarded manifestation of the real struggles I am not okay letting out. Over the years, I've gotten better at acknowledging that I am not always okay.

For one, I have had a tough time adjusting my parenting style based on the unique personalities of my kids. It is hard when all of the tactics you thought would help your kids seem altogether ineffective. That has been my reality the last couple of years. The developmental milestones, age appropriate hobbies, and disciplinary methods that work for most kids have not worked for ours. I have beat myself up countless times. This has made me feel like a failure more times than I know how to count. It's easy to seclude oneself and never admit you are struggling. It seemed like I was the only dad in this zone. Thankfully my community of friends is filled with good listeners. They are more like brothers. I have been able to share my life (good parts and bad) and know they will pray for us. They will pray for my wife, my sons, and my daughter. They will encourage me and love me even in the midst of my insecurities. This is what we all need.

Everyone needs a safe place not to be okay. Not just men and not just women—everyone. Kids too. God created us with needs, the biggest of which is Jesus. We are born with a need (our biggest need). He created us with a need to literally place our faith and trust in a Man Who died over 2000 years ago in order to be in the right place in relationship to Him. We literally are in desperate need from the moment we enter this world. We are broken. We are a mess. Think about it like this: anything I can face as a dad, a husband, a man, or just a human is nothing compared to my need for Jesus. This frees me up from fearing vulnerability.

A bird's-eye view shows me I'm not okay. You're not okay. We are all living in the messiness of life, and we all have the same basic needs. Wouldn't life be easier if you had a place to be vulnerable and open with people? Do you have a group of friends you trust and know would love you, pray for you, and walk with you through your mess? And would you gladly walk alongside them in their mess? People relate to realness. If you think someone isn't walking through a mess, they are lying. Everyone has baggage. Find your community and safe space; then be willing to admit when you are not okay.

The Bravest Thing I've Ever Done - Laura

It's important to rest and spend time alone with God. However, it's risky to use that as a hiding place. God designed us to feel encouragement and validation when we are connected with people at different stages of their faith. Without realizing it, it's easy to let our ego lead when we are hurting. That means you approach each relationship hoping for personal gain. We seek some type of affirmation that we are as awesome as we think we are. On the opposite end, it is equally egotistical to consider yourself worthless and undeserving of real connection. God didn't create you to be a hermit. Using your emotions to justify solitude will only create more darkness. I speak from personal experience.

Never in my younger years had I been a high anxiety or melancholy person. Throughout childhood we had some family rough patches when my dad had cancer, but we all kept a level head (or so it seemed from my perspective). Graduating from high school, I was still pretty even keel. I've been accused of being unrealistically optimistic. I was the bubbly positive girl you saw bouncing through the dorm hallways. It actually sounds both endearing and equally annoying to describe myself that way.

Things changed when I became a mom. And again. And then again. After our third little bambino surprised us, those pregnancy hormones not only changed my body but also my mental health. I became depressed. This was all unfamiliar to me, and I felt like my whole life was in a fishbowl. I'd smile and nod at people with my eyes glazed over. I'd wonder if they could see my thoughts and sense the darkness I felt. The boys would ask me to play, and I'd tell them I didn't have it in me. They'd ask me why I was crying while I put them to bed. I felt like a shell, walking around dragging myself through the days. Nick knew something was off. I knew something was off. I couldn't talk myself out of this deep hole. I wanted to sleep and cry all day.

Through this process, it was very easy to push people out. I'd get texts or phone calls and ignore them. We'd have work events I couldn't miss, so I'd put on my fake smile and cry myself to sleep that night, utterly exhausted from mingling. The first step in the right direction was admitting how I felt. Admitting that even though I felt crazy, I wasn't. Admitting that something was not right, and it wasn't something I should be ashamed of or could even control. This cycle continued on and off for over a year. I could sense myself climbing out and then falling back in. Raising three littles—treading water with a newborn, a middle child who was regressing, and a defiant kindergartner—was too much for this mom to handle. Of course I had no desire to interact with friends and adults or any other human for that matter. I wanted to be invisible because being visible was too hard.

I will never forget the day I called to make an appointment with a therapist. It was International Women's Day. As my social media newsfeed filled up with memes of strong women, quotes about being powerful, and stories of heroism, I was suddenly aware of how incapable I was on my own. Let me be clear. I had zero desire to stand up and declare, "I am Jane. Hear me roar." I had played those cards before and found them to be inauthentic. I only wanted Jesus. I knew that when I admit I'm weak, I can then fully rely on His strength.

The bravest thing I've ever done was to google "Christian

counselors near me" and make that phone call. The second bravest thing was telling my husband. Nick has always been supportive of me and my waves of inspiration, yet it was embarrassing to admit that I couldn't get it together. Because of the stigma associated with such a choice, I believed that using our family budget on these weekly therapy sessions would be irresponsible. I did it anyway. This is what you do when you hit rock bottom. If you were less prideful than I am, you likely made a similar call before hitting rock bottom. That was wise.

The irony is not lost on me that the first thing my therapist recommended was to "get out of the house." I am a homebody. My home is my safe space. Yet she recognized that I was using it as a scapegoat, as if I had put a ball and chain around my own ankles while holding the key in my right hand. I didn't want to hear that though. I came to her because I wanted guidance on living behind my wall, not coming out from behind it. Nevertheless, she was telling me to tear the wall down. Was this a conspiracy? Had Nick paid her to tell me this?

Okay, I decided to play along and pretend she was right. Where would I go? Who would I see? I didn't have time to craft a closing argument as a rebuttal to her challenge, so I was willing to give it a shot. That next week I made some plans and went out with girlfriends. It felt nice. The next week I braved the grocery store with my three littles. That may have caused me to regress a bit. The more I opened my door, the more freedom I felt. For months I had felt alone, and almost instantly I could feel the sunshine on my soul.

God's Word tells us to "bear the burdens" of others (Galatians 6:2), but He also wants us to allow others to carry our burdens. When we spend time together with other believers, allowing them into our lives, we experience vulnerability and connection. Now, after a lot of work on myself and an infusion of courage from my friends, I first check my relationship pulse whenever I feel off. Have I been hiding? Or have I been willing to open up and do life with others? My encouragement to you is to open up your minds, hearts, and front doors.

> Community is God's desire for us—and a sign of a mature faith. Because at the end of the day, when we grow in our relationships with others, we're growing in relationship with Him![8]

To love fast and live slow when you are not okay is to allow others believers to carry your burdens and do life with you. .

CHAPTER SIXTEEN

Letting Sin Win

*"I do not understand what I do. For what I want to do I do
not do, but what I hate I do" (Romans 7:15).*

If you've made it this far, you know that I (Nick) have a
temper, you know that I'm stubborn, you know that I'm
prideful and that I've been a failure in a lot of areas in my
life. Sounds terrible, right? It's real. Most of us, if we are
honest, will admit that we are not perfect and have many
flaws. The difference between someone who overcomes
versus someone who gives in to sin is rooted in self-control.
Rather than give you more examples from my own life about
letting sin win, of which there are plenty, let's look at a guy
from the Bible.

In Matthew 19:16-22, a rich young man approaches Jesus,
asking what good thing he can do to get into heaven. Jesus
basically tells him to keep the commandments (referring to
the Ten Commandments). Things get interesting when the
rich young man asks Jesus which commandments. This is
Jesus's response:

"'Which ones?' he inquired. Jesus replied, 'You shall not murder, you shall not commit adultery, you shall not steal, you shall not give false testimony, honor you father and mother' and 'love your neighbor as yourself'" (Matthew 19:18-19).

Interestingly, Jesus only mentions the commands involving man in a physical sense. Nothing was mentioned about honoring God. I think Jesus did this because He knew the guy's heart was in a bad place. The rich young man, obviously arrogant, responds by telling Jesus he has kept all of these commandments. Hold on a second. I would've interrogated, "You've never disrespected your mom or dad? Never stolen a pencil or told a lie? You've never had a neighbor that you just couldn't stand?"

Thankfully, Jesus is much wiser than I am. Also, He is much more patient. He goes straight to the heart of the matter with love and compassion.

"Jesus answered, 'If you want to be perfect, go, sell your possessions and give to the poor, and you will have treasure in heaven. Then come, follow me'" (Matthew 19:21).

No one asked about being perfect. The man asked how to get to heaven. Yet Jesus was addressing a much deeper issue. He was addressing the heart. Knowing perfection is unattainable, sans Jesus, the conversation shifted from "What good thing can I do?" to "What good thing can I follow?" Getting into heaven is not about acceptable behavior, kind actions, or good choices; it's a heart issue.

This guy really thought he was good enough. Talk about some deep-seated pride. His response below said even more about where he was spiritually.

"When the young man heard this, he went away sad, because he had great wealth" (Matthew 19:22).

His stuff had more value to him than his eternal state. He obviously believed there was a real heaven because he asked Jesus how to get there. However, this man let sin win because he wouldn't follow Jesus no matter the cost. In every situation, isn't that what it means to let sin win? We choose what we want over what Jesus wants. Letting sin win means placing more value on the object of the sin than we place on Jesus. If we are not careful, choosing sin in the little things can have a ripple effect for greater sin.

The Ripple Effect of One Bad (Impulsive) Choice - Laura
I ran from the cops one time. No, it's not one of my proudest moments. But one thing led to another, and I soon found myself in a tangled novel of lies. Once I made the decision to push the gas pedal down, I had to commit to either rebellion or surrender. I'm not naturally rebellious, but I am naturally stubborn. To this day, I don't know what got into me. I was in high school; I can blame it on immaturity. Although I knew good and well what I was supposed to do, I did not do it. I suppose I was more fearful of getting caught than going to jail. Our reasoning can be so off when we are faced with the consequences of our actions. In that momentary lapse of judgment, I chose to go head-to-head with the highway authority. It was a bad choice.

Most bad decisions are impulsive. More often than not, we know right from wrong, but we still choose the wrong. Perhaps it's exhilarating. Perhaps your friends chose the wrong path and haven't gotten caught yet. Perhaps you think you are the exception to the rule. Whatever the reason may be, once you start lying to cover up your bad choice, you have to cover that lie with another lie and another lie. You will find yourself deep in a hole of deception. All endorphins from the original rush will quickly vanish. All you will have left is the heaviness of the mess you just made and the people you hurt along the way.

I bet you are wondering what happened next? Well, it gets worse. I saw the cop car hiding on the side of the road, I checked my speedometer, and my lead foot had done it again. I was a good 10 miles over the speed limit (okay, fine, it was 15 over). I was doomed. I slowed my driving and looked in my rear view mirror just in time to see his lights turn on. Was I ready to face the consequences and pay up? Apparently not. Just a few weeks prior, my friends had joked about getting out of a ticket because they kept driving and made some quick turns before the cop could get behind them. They beat the system. In a split second I decided to give it a shot. By "give it a shot" I mean succeed or the consequences would be far greater than a ticket. What the heck, it was dark, it was late, it's been done before, so it can be done again.

That was the first of many bad choices in this descent. I hit the gas pedal and scurried to find a turn-off road. None in sight. The cop had not yet come over the hill, so I still had a small chance of succeeding in Operation Runaway. Right around the corner, I spotted a driveway. Not my best option, but I was limited. I made a sharp turn.

Why is it that time seems to stand still when we are afraid? Second bad decision, pulling into a stranger's driveway. At this point I didn't even recognize myself. Who was this Laura making these instinctive choices? The Laura I knew was a rule follower. She was a straight-A student, homecoming queen, leader in her church youth group, and daughter of a well-respected family. Where was this anarchy coming from? I didn't have time to have these internal therapy sessions. I only had time to hide. I pulled into a side parking spot in the gravel driveway and turned off my headlights.

My heart was pounding as I looked down at my hands, "What have you made me do?" But my hands weren't leading this sting. My fear of being caught speeding had led to this elusive operation. I knew the entire maneuver was wrong. It was outside of my character, but I was in too deep now. Unaware that I had not been breathing, I let out my breath slowly as if fearing that someone might hear me. The cop's headlights passed by my driveway hideout. *No way. Did this really work? I will never do that again. What an idiot I am!*

Watching his car pass the driveway filled me with hope. But watching through the trees as his break lights slammed on filled me with horror. Third bad decision, not turning off my parking lights.

This is it, I told myself. You're going to jail. Why didn't you turn off the parking lights, Laura? If you were going to run, you should have done it right. You spent your whole life trying to do what's right, and in an instant, you screwed it all up.

I am not sure if God turned up the heat in my car or if I was having a mild panic attack, but I began to sweat. I finally turned off my parking lights—60 seconds too late. I was ready to face my inevitable fate. The cop pulled into the driveway, I got out of my car, and we were face-to-face.

Not ready to surrender, rebel Laura was still swinging with ideas. Fourth bad decision, she lied to the officer.

"Um, hi, officer, is everything okay?"

"You tell me. It looks like you are trying to run from the police. Is that correct?"

"What? No, sir. This is my friend's house. I stopped to say bye before I leave for college next week."

"You know the residents of this home, ma'am?"

"Yes, sir."

Lies. All lies. I had never stepped foot in that driveway before, nor did I know who was on the other side of the front door. But I soon found out.

"Okay. I was looking for you because you were doing 51 in a 35 speed zone. Are you aware you were speeding?"

"I am so sorry, officer. I didn't realize this road had a 35-mile-per-hour speed limit. I didn't see any signs. I'll slow down next time."

As if on cue, a young girl emerged from the back of the house. The family inside was sure to see the spiraling police lights streaming in their front windows. Oh, boy, this was a mess. One lie led to another and another and another that I was embarrassed to admit. I continued my chronicle and acted like I knew the young girl.

I shouted to her, "Hey, I'm sorry for all this. I will explain everything. Don't worry. Everything is okay. Just go back inside." And before coming any closer, she nodded in confusion and walked back inside.

I can't make this stuff up. It's shocking what lies and deceit we can create when we don't want to face the reality of the consequences we deserve. Sure, I felt a hint of conviction throughout this escapade, but it was buried deep under the need to not go to jail. Once I decided I didn't want to be held to the same road standards as every other law-abiding citizen, I had to put forth ten times the effort and stress to cover my tracks than if I had just surrendered.

We do this to God, too. We know what we should do, but we look for every other angle. We don't want to impose on our luxury, so we don't tithe. We don't want to face rejection, so we don't share the gospel. We don't want to feel conviction, so we deny our sins. One thing leads to another, and before we know it, we are in a stranger's driveway lying to a police officer and hoping to make it home without handcuffs. Oh, is that just me? Per usual.

Once this confused young girl walked back in her house, the police officer proceeded to give me a ticket. I've never been happier to receive that piece of carbon copy paper. A ticket? I was walking away with only a ticket. I should have felt like a champion, but I was burning inside. When we both got in our cars, I took a deep breath. My hands were shaking, and I vowed never to do something so stupid again. As I cranked my car, I noticed that the officer was still in the driveway. Was he changing his mind? Was this a test?

It took about four seconds before I realized he was calling me on my bluff. He wanted to see if I really knew these people. One way or another, I had to confront my lie head on. If I was brave enough to run, hide, and lie to a police officer, I had to be brave enough to knock on a stranger's front door and apologize for the commotion I had caused in their front yard.

I turned off my car, opened my driver's side door, and walked up to the front patio of this stranger's house with my head hung low. I was ready to out myself. Knock, knock, knock. The cop pulled out of the driveway. Here goes nothing. Knock, knock, knock. I hoped they would open the door and allow me to air my grievances since the entire incident was heavy on my conscience by now. But no one came to the door. I don't blame them. I was a crazy girl who had brought the cops to their front yard and yelled at them to go back inside. I'd be scared of me too. Actually, I was scared of me. I was scared of who I had become when I let sin win. God displayed a beautiful story of mercy toward me that night. I deserved much more than a ticket and some token embarrassment.

When We Let Sin Win - Nick

Oh, boy am I thankful that we serve a merciful and gracious God. Letting sin win can result in immediate destruction if not for the grace of God. Just as Jesus taught the rich young man that it was not about doing but about his heart's condition, so our chance to honor God and do the right thing is not external. God doesn't want us to walk through life bound by a book of laws. He wants us to accept the new way of living in the Spirit.

As a matter of fact, the more we focus on rule following and staying within the lines, the more attention we give to the temptation. Have you ever been riding a bike and seen a rock in front of you? If you stare at the rock hoping to avoid it, your bike will inevitably steer toward that obstacle instead of away from the potential danger. You gravitate towards your fixation. Paul says, "the law aroused these evil desires that produce a harvest of sinful deeds" (Romans 7:5, NLT). Sure, we all hope to have enough self-control to avoid succumbing to temptation, but we are human. God is the One Who gives us the ability to "produce a harvest of good deeds" for Him (Romans 7:4). Within ourselves, we are not strong enough to combat the pressures of the world.

Once we release the powerful grip of legalism (dependence on moral law rather than on personal religious faith[9]), we can seek the freedom Paul talks about in Romans 7.

"Now [that] we have been released from the law, for we died to it and are no longer captive to its power. Now we can serve God, not in the old way of obeying the letter of the law, but in the new way of living in the Spirit" (Romans 7:6).

Many would like to think that this means we are free to do as we please. Didn't Paul say we have been released from the old law and its strict restrictions? Didn't he say "there is none righteous, no not one" (Romans 3:10, KJV)? Since that is the case, shouldn't we have permission to live as we see fit? Humankind is tangled in an array of differing moral codes. We have basic laws accepted by the majority that keep our communities governed, but what about other guidelines that are more fluid? Are we free to interpret what is approved by God?

Since Jesus came to earth, died on the cross, and broke the curse of death, changing the course of history, we ought not focus on what borderline things we are *allowed* to do but rather on what He'd want us to do to honor that sacrifice. Our whole life should be a giant thank you letter to Jesus. We should be in constant pursuit to please Him and make Him known. First Corinthians 6:12 summarizes well the topic of what is allowed or not.

> "You say, 'I am allowed to do anything'—but not
> everything is good for you. And even though 'I am
> allowed to do anything,' I must not become a slave to
> anything."

Once an activity, item, person or even good deed replaces God's rightful number one spot in your life, it becomes an idol. You are now living to serve that idol and have become a slave all over again. Jesus died to set us free. He didn't die to put us on a leash of conviction or a path of ever-changing ethics; He died on the cross to give us eternal life. There was a massive canyon between us and eternal life, and He bridged the gulf. We've all let sin win at times, which should give us more reason to appreciate grace and mercy.

> "Thanks be to God that, though you used to be
> slaves to sin, you have come to obey from your heart
> the pattern of teaching that has now claimed your
> allegiance. You have been set free from sin and have
> become slaves to righteousness" (Romans 6:17-18).

**To love fast and live slow is to resist the temptation to
sin, but when we do, to walk in freedom, knowing His
grace and mercies are real.**

CHAPTER SEVENTEEN

Letting Hope Win

"Preparing your minds for action, and being sober-minded,
set your hope fully on the grace that will be
brought to you at the revelation of Jesus Christ"
(1 Peter 1:13, ESV).

I (Laura) think most of us can agree that the holidays are special. We all have our favorites. Some of us may walk through them with sadness and bittersweet reflection, while others dance through the days with unbridled joy. Wherever you are in your holiday prowess, can we all agree that they bring anticipated celebration? You go to bed with butterflies in your stomach because by the time you wake up, the world will be transformed. Many rules and boundaries are lifted for those 24 hours. You may be able to hunt eggs and eat candy left on the ground, launch fireworks after bedtime, eat birthday cake with your hands, or open presents left under a glowing tree.

These rituals are not difficult to duplicate and could easily happen any other day of the year, but it wouldn't feel right. You can't celebrate Halloween on June 27. The neighbors wouldn't be prepared. You can't showcase Christmas decorations and lights on your lawn in April, although the year after our daughter was born, I am pretty sure we didn't take down our Christmas decorations until the end of February. You can certainly rewrite the social cues for holidays like we did; there are no formal rules against it, but it would take away the novelty.

Our sweet middle son, Everett, is a holiday hoarder. He is four years old, and he interrogates me each morning with the same series of questions. He asks me if it's Christmas. Every. Single. Day.

"No, sweetie, it's not Christmas yet."

Then he asks me, "Is it Easter?"

I hate to be the bearer of bad news. "No, Everett, it's not Easter today either."

He persists. "Is it Halloween tonight?" He goes on and on. We go through this dialogue for a while. Finally, one morning this week he asked, "Is it Mother's Day?"

And I made an executive decision not to let my little boy down again. "Yes, as a matter of fact. Yes, Everett. It can be Mother's Day! Every day is Mother's Day!" A girl can dream.

I see nothing wrong with looking forward to special days or a break from the daily grind. An interruption to the rhythm of a steady month can spice things up and help us come back stronger. Everett loves a change of pace. He's like his daddy. His hope for the holidays is adorable, all the more reason I feel bad telling him, "No buddy. It's just a Tuesday." He knows what he is looking forward to and wants it to come quickly. He wants it today. When he wakes up, he wants to open his eyes, knowing that what he's anticipated has arrived. Don't we all? There is something special in knowing that one day Christmas will arrive. The days pass, and time moves forward without waiting for permission. With only 365 days in a year, he trusts that one of the 365 times he asks, the right day will come, and I will gladly answer, "Yes, Everett! It's Christmas!"

Hope Defined - Laura

By definition, *hope* is "a feeling of expectation and desire for a certain thing to happen."[10] The world has a different interpretation of hope than God has. It's common to hope something goes your way. Let's replace the word *hope* with the word *wish*. It's common to wish something would go your way. You cross your fingers and want the outcome to be in your favor. There is uncertainty in the outcome, and the hope being described here is circumstantial. Oftentimes we hope for a kind word or a compliment. We fish around for validation and seek outside input for our security blanket.

I remember spending Thanksgiving in Orlando, Florida, with my family back in 1996. We all gathered around the small kitchen table in my parents' apartment. My mom went around the table and complimented each of our most endearing qualities. You know, good traditional stuff. She boasted about my sister's self-discipline and kind heart. She showered my brother with compliments about his creativity. As she went around the table, my brain swam with endorphins. I had hoped she'd decorate me with unparalleled compliments. *What will she come up with? What parts of my amazingness will she elevate first? Academic Doogie Howser? Mother Teresa compassion? Multi-tasking jedi?*

No. None of it.

She grinned and said, "And Laura, your stubbornness is your biggest attribute."

What? What does that mean? That's all you've got? I visualized a mule. A stubborn mule. A donkey. An ass. My tenderhearted mom had just called me an ass. I had no comeback. I said thanks, and we ate our turkey.

Much like what happened on that Thanksgiving etched in my memory bank forever, when we hope for something to build us up, we are often dropkicked. I've never heard my mom say a foul word about anyone on the planet, and I know she meant no harm. Stubbornness and endurance can absolutely be admirable traits when used for the right cause. My mistake was hoping for something to fill my void.

On the contrary, the hope that God talks about does fill our void. As believers, we should hold onto hope that God will fulfill His promises. There is no doubt or circumstance that could change the outcome. Our hope is placed in the solidity of the future. Without hope, we'd turn inward to resolve our problems. We'd become even more selfish and neglect to live out this love fast mission. We no longer have to carry concern about our destiny or live in anxiety as if we are solely responsible for our future. We put our hope in what the Bible tells us is to come. A well-known theologian, John Piper, describes hope like this:

> If we don't have the hope that Christ is for us, then we will be engaged in self-preservation and self-enhancement. But if we let ourselves be taken care of by God for the future—whether five minutes or five centuries from now—then we can be free to love others. Then God's glory will shine more clearly, because that's how He becomes visible.[11]

Oftentimes when I see block quotes like the one above, I skim over them. (This is especially true of long passages of Scripture because I can read the summary and application in the subsequent paragraph. Just keeping it real.) If you are like me and skimmed over the above quote, do me a favor: go read the one above. I'll wait; go ahead.

These words really spoke to me. God becomes visible when He shines more clearly through us. In a dark and confused world where people are looking for resolve to their distress, we are the instruments God chooses to shine His hope to others. If we let go of our angst and let God control the future, we are free to love fast. Biblical hope is trusting that God has your best in mind. Trust that you can wake up each morning, put on your love fast live slow mindset, and then let God do His thing. You don't have to play god. You don't have to nail down a 10-year plan. How about taking off those shackles and living for today. Once you place your hope in Jesus, you are free. Free to love fast, live slow and enjoy the ride.

Don't Fall for the Counterfeit

The part that gets me is the waiting. I make mistakes and fall for counterfeits when I am waiting. Our son Everett has to wait weeks before the next major holiday rolls around. He knows it's coming but has to wade through the less exciting days of the month. This in-between time is important. It's where discipline and maturity collide. While waiting for God to give us our next best step, it's easy for the Enemy to dive in and sabotage the process. How many times have you prayed for a clear answer or direction, and all of a sudden you have four times the options in front of you?

Distraction is one of Satan's strategic ploys. He knows you are chasing after God and your hope in God would present a big threat to his evil plans, so he throws you for a loop. He allures you away with subtle impatience, greed, vanity, or pride. But when we place our hope in God's plans for our future, we must wait and not become sidetracked by false hope. This waiting period is where God wants to teach us what's real and what's fake. He is real. What the world offers is fake. Simple but, oh, so hard.

I'm not a shopper or a collector of fancy things, so I wouldn't be able to identify a luxury knockoff if I saw one. But I know there are a lot of counterfeits in the world. There are high end purses, jewelry, and technology that are duplicated all the time. They are just slightly different—unique enough to avoid being sued but subtle enough to sell to an eager or gullible buyer. I read recently that counterfeiting goods has become a $461 million problem.[12] It's a big deal apparently. And even more apparent is the obvious demand for counterfeit items in the marketplace.

Knowing this happens shouldn't shock me. Oftentimes the phony items are cheaper and easier to come by. The appearance can be misleading until you take a closer look. We live in a deceptive world. It can be tricky to decipher what's real. Nick is my sounding board. I do not pride myself on having excellent discernment. Thus far in our marriage, Nick has had a 100% track record as it relates to cautioning me about a person or situation. Even still, sometimes we aren't sure about which direction, which purchase, or which decision God wants us to make. God never purposely leads us down a counterfeit road, but He can certainly allow it to provide us with life lessons along the way. When I ask for guidance, sometimes I listen; sometimes I don't. And I've walked into many sticky situations because I took my eyes off God.

Be on the Winning Team - Nick

The Bible tells the story of a guy named Elijah who was a prophet God used to give messages to Israel's king, Ahab. Elijah was a devout man, an obedient follower of God. Countless times he saw God work and move amongst his people, and at times he, himself, was the catalyst for miracles from God. Seriously, go read all about him in the book of 1 Kings when you get a chance.

In 1 Kings 18, God sent Elijah to King Ahab to confront the king about his abandonment of the worship of God for the worship of Baal and Asherah. He told king Ahab to have all of the people of Israel and all of the prophets of Baal and Asherah meet him on Mount Carmel. There were 450 prophets of Baal and 400 prophets of Asherah assembled when Elijah issued a challenge. The story gets really great here. He basically had a competition of the prophets in front of everyone. He had them create an altar and then call upon the god they believed in to send fire to consume the offering on the altar.

Naturally, Elijah allowed the 850 false prophets to go first. They were crying out and doing all sorts of crazy things to try to get something to happen at their altar, but nothing did. Elijah started taunting a bit, saying things like "Maybe your God is taking a nap" or "Maybe he's traveling." His taunting actually made the false prophets do even crazier things. They began to cut themselves and shout louder and louder. Nothing happened. Nothing.

Let's pause the crescendo of suspense for a bit. I think a lot of us have put our hope in all of the wrong things at one point or another. Maybe your hope is in the wrong thing now. These prophets had put all of their hope in something that was never going to succeed. They believed in a counterfeit god. But if hope is going to win, that hope has to be in something certain. To hope means there is an expectation of fulfillment.

When I was a kid, my brother and I used to have crazy aspirations of building forts in the woods, hunting our own food, and sleeping in the forts we had built. Bamboo grew in the woods all around our house, and we would try to make bows and arrows with it, as well as build bridges over the creek and treehouses in the trees. We called our woods Sherwood Forest because we loved Robin Hood. As a kid, there is a lot more hope in our minds than when we become adults. My brother and I had a certainty in our minds that we could do these things. But with the limited materials, resources, and experience we had, our hope was misplaced.

What we should've done was ask our dad for help or ideas on how to accomplish these tasks or if they were even realistic with our space and resources. We could have had actual hope with our dad involved. What we had wasn't hope at all. It was just wishes.

In order for hope to win, our hope has to be placed in the right area or areas. If Jesus is at the center of all we plan to do, we'll be alright. We can believe with an expectation that things will work out, and even if they don't (and sometimes they won't), we can know that our motives were good and move on. This isn't to discourage you. It's actually the opposite. Dream big, plan big, dive deep, and believe! Just remember that in the end, if what you do doesn't involve people seeing more of Jesus, there's no hope in it for others. Let's let hope win in us so that we can give hope to others. I want to see others have hope. I want my friends to be successful. Life is not a competition with those around us. It's a competition against an Enemy that would see us all fail if he could.

So what happened with that competition of the prophets? After the 850 prophets gave up, Elijah had the altar of God rebuilt and prepared it for an offering. There are details I won't go into here because I want you to read the whole story for yourself, but I will tell you that Elijah had gallons and gallons of water poured over the altar after it was prepared. He dug a large trench around the altar, and there was so much water that it filled the trench. Then Elijah prayed this prayer:

> "O LORD, God of Abraham, Isaac, and Israel, let it be known this day that you are God in Israel, and that I am your servant, and that I have done all these things at your word. Answer me, O LORD, answer me, that this people may know that you, O LORD, are God, and that you have turned their hearts back" (1 Kings 18: 36-37).

This was a prayer of hope. He believed God would work. And he wanted hope to win, not just for the "contest" between the false prophets and himself but for all the people of Israel. Look at the last part of the prayer. "That this people may know that you...are God" was his goal. Hope wins when we want others to have the hope of Jesus. Now go read 1

Kings 18 and see how God answers Elijah's prayer. Seriously, put this book down and go see what happens.

To love fast and live slow is to team up with the winning team, God. He is all the hope we need.

CHAPTER EIGHTEEN

Letting Others Win

*"Greater love has no one than this: to lay
down one's life for one's friends" (John 15:13).*

L etting hope win only works when we are willing to let
others win. If my (Nick) *numero uno* priority is making
sure I come out on top every time, I probably am more concerned with myself than with others. If that's the case, others
have little room in my life. Being a dad of two boys (and a
girl), there is no shortage of opportunities for competition in
our home. Maybe it's just a friendly game of Uno or Go Fish
or perhaps laser tag. The point is, I have constant opportunities to teach and learn the concept of letting others win.

My boys are now seven and five. EVERYTHING is a
competition to be won in their little minds. The funny thing
is, I have to be careful because I sometimes feed their competitive natures by my example or actions. I don't always let
them win at games because they need to learn to lose with
grace just as much as they learn to win with it. I'm not sure
how it got to be that way, but I think it's called life. I am the
same way. I have a very competitive nature. I tell people often
that I hate losing more than I love winning. Think about that.

For me, winning for the sake of winning isn't the goal. It's not being a loser. How jacked up is that? I hate the sting of losing more than I love the joy of winning. I still have to work on grace in my nature when it comes to winning and losing.

Letting others win is not always a matter of personally losing. Letting others win has more to do with our attitude toward ourselves than an attitude toward others. One of my favorite books in the Bible is Philippians. Paul paints a beautiful, poetic picture for us in chapter two that is one of my favorite passages in the entire Bible and has really become a life verse passage to me. I strive to live by these verses every day.

"So if there is any encouragement in Christ, any comfort from love, any participation in the Spirit, any affection and sympathy, complete my joy by being of the same mind, having the same love, being in full accord and of one mind. Do nothing from selfish ambition or conceit, but in humility count others more significant than yourselves. Let each of you look not only to his own interests, but also to the interests of others. Have this mind among yourselves, which is yours in Christ Jesus, who, though he was in the form of God, did not count equality with God a thing to be grasped, but emptied himself, by taking the form of a servant, being born in the likeness of men. And being found in human form, he humbled himself by becoming obedient to the point of death, even death on a cross. Therefore God has highly exalted him and bestowed on him the name that is above every name, so that at the name of Jesus every knee should bow, in heaven and on earth and under the earth, and every tongue confess that Jesus Christ is Lord, to the glory of God the Father" (Philippians 2:1-11).

The concept here is simple. If we are in tune with Jesus, we will be unified with other believers, and we will put others before ourselves because that is the example that Jesus set for us to live by. And if we do that, everything points to Jesus so that He is glorified and lifted up for all to see. When we let others win, it isn't about a competition at all. It is about how we view and treat others...as if they are created in God's image and we owe them the same grace God shows us. It's not always easy to look at people through the lenses that God expects us to look at them through. I imagine it was not so easy for Jesus to remain quiet when He was accused and questioned so many times by Pharisees and lawyers.

I had a youth pastor when I was in high school who was one of the best examples of Jesus I have ever been around. I won't go into details about what happened, but during the time that he was my student pastor, their family was deeply hurt by a neighbor, so much so that the neighbor went to prison. In the midst of my student pastor's dealing with the pain and suffering over what had happened and getting some necessary help, the neighbor's yard began to grow and was becoming an eyesore. My student pastor lived out the verses above. He thought of the best way he could still show this neighbor the love of Jesus, even though he had been crushed by the hurt that this neighbor had caused his family. So he went and began cutting his neighbor's grass. He never stopped pursuing the legal ramifications of the neighbor's actions from a legal perspective, but he resolved that this neighbor was going to see the gospel and forgiveness even in the midst of all that had happened.

This story is an example of letting others win. Knowing that the most important thing people can get from us is the message of Jesus and the cross, we need to communicate to others that their lives matter and that they are loved by God and by us. Paul basically tells us that if we want to win, let others win.

Do What Jesus Did - Laura

It blows my mind that Jesus lived every day selflessly. I mean, I know He's Jesus, but if we really boil down all the passive, selfish things we do in a 24-hour period, it's nauseating. Could you count on two hands how many times a day you subconsciously consider yourself more important than others? I'll bring up the most obvious trigger: being in a hurry. When we are in a hurry, we can easily turn into monsters. Everyone is in our way. Everyone is taking too long. Everything is working against us. Woe is me. Rushing to school, work, the store…living a rushed life is surely the best litmus test to our heart's truest condition.

There isn't a number large enough to calculate the times I've chosen my own self-interest above others. Yet Jesus was fully human and managed to put others first every moment during his 33 years on earth. My heart desires to be more like Jesus, but I cannot comprehend the discipline it requires to set aside my desires for every other human on the planet. Perhaps *discipline* is the wrong word. Jesus did not lack discipline, that's for sure. It wasn't a bucketful of self-control that equipped Him to let others win; it was His unfiltered love for us. By us, I mean every human on the planet.

Do you love every human on the planet? Sure, some of us dust off conviction by justifying that we don't know everyone on the planet. True. But of the people we do know, do we know their needs? Do we care? I bet you do care. You seem like a decent enough person (since by choice you are reading a book about Jesus and love). However, life is busy. Life is distracting. Speedbumps get us off pace, and we spend a lot of energy trying to get back on track.

Jesus also lived through speed bumps. We don't know much about his first 30 years, except that He "lived obediently" (Luke 2:51). And the last three years of His life were documented by others who observed Him and followed His teachings. It only took three years of His beautiful life to teach us everything we need to know about how to treat others.

The idea of letting others win isn't based on a strategic game of Monopoly (a family favorite), where you intentionally neglect buying Boardwalk so your opponents won't be out more money for rent. I'm sure we have some competitive readers who wouldn't dare let their kid beat them every round. The same is true for you and me. We don't have to win every round. We don't have to get all the credit. We don't have to steal that closest parking spot (I can hear Nick cringe). We don't have to be thanked every day for cleaning the house (this one stings; now I am cringing). We don't have to one-up every achievement. We don't have to post the most eloquent picture and swipe down 400 times to update the likes. We don't have to belittle someone's compliment toward us by denying it's true. After all, refusing a compliment is like asking for it twice.

What I am trying to get across is this, when was the last

time you purposely put yourself last? Jesus did not neglect self-care or idolize *asceticism*. For those who feel like asceticism is a big word, I just googled it too. *Asceticism* is "severe self-discipline and avoidance of all forms of indulgence, typically for religious reasons."[13] Yes, that's an actual thing. But it's not our thing. God has not called us to give up every personal desire. However, we are called to be like Jesus and "[He] laid down His life for us. And we ought to lay down our life for our brothers" (1 John 3:16).

Letting others win is that small fork in the road where you have to decide whether you want to go the easier route or the route that will positively impact the most people. Consider the eternal ripple effect of following your air tight schedule versus allowing interruptions and real-life conversations. When we let others win, we let others in. We are fed the lie that we have too much to do and too little time to do it. God only assigns us what we are able to accomplish each day. If you have too much on your plate, who is filling it up? If we are too busy for people and relationships, then what is the point of our life here on earth? Life is meant to be shared.

Even in the perfection of Eden, before the fall of man, God said, "It is not good for man to be alone" (Genesis 2:18). Did you know the word "together" is mentioned in the Bible 484 times? That's more than "do not fear" is mentioned and more than "wisdom" is mentioned and more than "pray" is mentioned, all of which are highly important. Why would God include the idea of togetherness so frequently in the Bible? It's because He created us to live, work, serve, play, and grow with others. In the book *The Purpose Driven Life*, Rick Warren says,

"The Bible says we are put together, joined together, built together, members together, heirs together, fitted together, and held together and will be caught up together."[14]

That seems to cover all the bases. It would be nice to live in a togetherness fantasyland where everyone got along, connected on deep levels, shared in empathy, and carried each other's burdens, but God created us with limits. There is no way we can befriend every person on the planet. Jesus was the kindest of them all yet only connected deeply with twelve.

I'd say my capacity is similar to that of Jesus. I try to be friendly and smiley to everyone I meet, but I have a true sisterhood that is small in number. Among my small group of closest friends, I want to let them win by asking how I can pray for them. I want to let them win by offering to watch their kids for a date night. I want to let them win by listening to their pain with zero judgment. I want to let them win by celebrating their good days even during my bad days. The Enemy is sneaky and will do whatever it takes to bring down your army. If you hold bitterness or envy in your heart because fellow believers are walking on sunshine, then you aren't letting them win. If all is going right in their world and you can't catch a break, be happy for them anyway. Celebrate their successes and trust that God knows what He is doing with your story. The more you love others, the more you tell the world that Jesus is real.

"Your strong love for each other will prove to the world that you are my disciples" (John 13:35, TLB).

"Whenever we have the opportunity, we should do good to everyone" (Galatians 6:10, NLT).

"Use every chance you have for doing good" (Ephesians 5:16, NCV).

"Whenever you possibly can, do good to those who need it. Never tell your neighbors to wait until tomorrow if you can help them now" (Proverbs 3:27-28, GNTA).

To love fast and live slow is to set aside your personal preferences in order to bless others.

⌒⌒

CONCLUSION

Everything we go through is a character building opportunity. When you face opposition, the world is going to
see what you are really all about. The quickest way to measure
a person's motives is to watch when they are squeezed by
hardships. What comes out? A selfish attitude, an ungrateful
spirit, a hurtful argument? Or a patient mind, an open hand,
and a compassionate response? What we put into our minds
will naturally come out. If we are surrounded with cynicism
and judgment, those mindsets will rub off on us. You are not
immune to those influences, and neither are we. If we fall
victim to the marketing that more is better and fast is best,
we won't give ourselves the chance to experience the peace
of living slow.

We see a major flaw in today's culture, and we want to
transform it.

God wants us to reflect on good things (Philippians 4:8).
God wants us to use our time wisely (Psalm 90:12). God
wants us to forget the past and look forward to what lies
ahead (Philippians 3:13). God wants us to call on Him when
we are in trouble, and He wants to rescue us (Psalm 50:15).
God wants us to be careful what we think because our thoughts shape our life (Proverbs 4:23). God wants us to slow
down and wait patiently for Him (Psalm 37:7). God doesn't

want you just to pretend to love others; He wants you to really love them (Romans 12:9). There will never be a day when you have finally *arrived* and reached the peak of this love fast and live slow marathon. No, it's a journey. It's a whole lot of self-reflection. It's laying down what you expected from life and asking God to pave your new path. And this will be the most life-giving adventure of your many trips around the sun.

There is no better way to end this book than to reflect on Jesus once again. For us to grasp the most important part of what Jesus has done for us requires an understanding why He did it. We are evil. I am evil. Apart from God, I can do nothing good. I was bound for destruction and separation from God without Jesus's coming into my life. I could live a life as a good person, and the world would look proudly upon me. I could help the homeless and cure diseases without ever taking a dime, and at the end of life, it would all mean nothing if I didn't know Jesus. So when we begin to understand that sin separates us from God, we can really begin to appreciate the gospel on a completely different level. Our identity is changed from the core. The gospel is not some shell that we place over a poorly configured life; instead, it is bringing life into a completely dead body and giving it divine purpose. How awesome is that? Our identity is literally to be Jesus to the world.

Loving God and others will force us to slow down, open our eyes, and make *love* a verb. We must look for the needs of others. We must appreciate the nuances of God's character in both the simple and the complex. We must pursue opportunities to unrush our lives, where we are able to look past ourselves and into the community God has given us to serve.

We must put to action the acts of kindness we wish someone would have done for us. We must drop the ego and work to make God famous, not ourselves.

You have the ability to define what loving fast and living slow means to you. Before you jump to your next activity, take a moment to reflect. What does it mean to you? How will you apply it to your life?

We'd love to know your story. Join us at *www.lovefastliveslow. com/takeaction* and tell us one thing you will do in the next week to apply these principles to your life. In the meantime, here are some updates that may provide closure to some of the cliffhangers in the book.

Even without her ID, Laura did get on the flight, seat 37A.

Nick still doesn't have a sailboat. Apparently he will have one soon though because Leland said he'd ask Santa for a boat next Christmas. That's how it works, right?

After Laura broke her arm, she became more involved in that Christian organization on campus, and that's where she met Nick.

Nick still loves camping. Now that we live in Florida, his chances of freezing to death have decreased.

That debt that was smothering us? We kissed it goodbye. Our house finally sold in February 2020, and we paid the debt off. I can't even believe I am writing that. Wow!

That friend Laura was mean to in middle school ended up becoming one of her best friends and was a bridesmaid in our wedding. God works all things out.

Nick loves the church, even after feeling burned by it. He has been working in church ministry for nearly two decades and has fresh eyes on how God restores relationships.

We've figured out a rhythm to raising our neurodiverse

family. Parenting is no cake walk, but we feel a peace about the tough school decisions we've made for the future.

Laura still has kopophobia. And she has never told her parents about running from the cops. Oops. No better time than now, right? Hi, Mom.

Lastly, we want to pray for you:

"God, we know you are there, always open-armed and ready for us to come to you in prayer. Thank you for leading these new friends to *Love Fast Live Slow*. May the stories and encouragement we've shared resonate with the deepest and most authentic parts of their hearts. We trust and believe You are pleased when we follow in Jesus's footsteps: to walk in love and live with our eyes open to the needs of others. We know this reflects who Jesus is. Amen."

LOVE FAST LIVE SLOW STATEMENTS
Take some time to reflect and meditate on these statements.

- To love fast and live slow is to follow Jesus's example and always love first (even when you are in a storm).

- To love fast and live slow in marriage is to give your spouse the best of you.

- To love fast and live slow in parenting is to raise your kids like God raises you (with patience and forgiveness).

- To love fast and live slow is to stop striving to prove yourself and instead surrender to who you are in Christ.

- To love fast and live slow within your community is to open up and break bread together.

- To love fast and live slow is to happily fulfill the responsibilities God has given you right now.

- To love fast and live slow is to let God be your one and only adventure Guide.

- To love fast and live slow when you are in need is to pray day and night and let God be God.

- To love fast and live slow as a follower of Jesus is to abide by His greatest commandment: love God and love people.

- To love fast and live slow with a big idea, be like Nehemiah. Pray, plan, have courage, and then take big

191

action.

- To love fast and live slow is to obey Him even if you feel unqualified.

- To love fast and live slow is to avoid gossip or slander and find ways to lift one another up.

- To love fast and live slow as you live outside the box, accept how God created you and delight in His creativity.

- To love fast and live slow is to surrender the urge to be all and do all. Take a deep, slow breath and follow God's lead and pace.

- To love fast and live slow when you are not okay is to allow others believers to carry your burdens and do life with you.

- To love fast and live slow is to resist the temptation to sin, but when we do, to walk in freedom, knowing His grace and mercies are real.

- To love fast and live slow is to team up with the winning team, God. He is all the hope we need.

- To love fast and live slow is to set aside your personal preferences in order to bless others.

NOTES

1. "Report: Americans Most Unhappy People in the World." *ABC 13 News*, February 20, 2013, https://abc13.com/archive/9000225/.

2. "Suicide Statistics." *Befrienders Worldwide*, June 1, 2010, https://www.befrienders.org/suicide-statistics.

3. "Feeling Safe in an Unsafe World." *Real Matters*, April 26, 2017, http://real-matters.com/?p=165.

4. David Lomas, *The Truest Thing about You: Identity, Desire, and Why It all Matters*. (Colorado Springs: David C. Cook, 2014).

5. *Merriam-Webster, s.v.* "follower," accessed July 7, 2019, https://www.merriam-webster.com/dictionary/follower.

6. *Merriam-Webster, s.v.* "narcissism," accessed July 7, 2019, https://www.merriam-webster.com/dictionary/narcissism.

7. Wayne S. Walker, "Nehemiah: A Cupbearer for the Lord," *The Expository Files*, August 2012, https://www.bible.ca/ef/topical-nehemiah-a-cupbearer-for-the-lord.htm.

8. "Bible Verses about Community." *Dave Ramsey*. https://www.daveramsey.com/blog/bible-verses-about-community.

9. *Merriam-Webster, s.v.* "legalism," accessed November 8, 2019, https://www.dictionary.com/browse/legalism.

10. *Merriam-Webster, s.v.* "hope," accessed July 23, 2019, https://www.merriam-webster.com/dictionary/hope.

11. John Piper, "What Is So Important about Christian Hope?" *Desiring God*, March 7, 2008, https://www.desiringgod.org/interviews/what-is-so-important-about-christian-hope.

12. Dawn Chardonnal, "Global Impacts of Counterfeiting

and Piracy to Reach US $4.2 Trillion by 2022," *International Chamber of Commerce (ICC),* June 6, 2017, https://iccwbo.org/media-wall/news-speeches/global-impacts-counterfeiting-piracy-reach-us4-2-trillion-2022/.

13. *Merriam-Webster, s.v.* "asceticism," accessed February 1, 2020, https://www.merriam-webster.com/dictionary/asceticism

14. Rick Warren, *The Purpose Driven Life: What on Earth Am I Here For?* (Grand Rapids, Michigan: Zondervan, 2002).

ABOUT THE AUTHORS

Nick and Laura Mendenhall are obsessed with pursuing a simple life that revolves around raising their family and loving their community. Nick has been working in ministry for almost two decades and can appreciate the tug-of-war between work and play. Laura is the author of best-selling eBook *Hidden Heroes: How God Uses Everyday People to Change the World*. Their years of experience speaking at events, writing Bible studies, and leading others in discipleship shines through their ministry at *Love Fast Live Slow*.

Nick and Laura both graduated from the University of West Georgia, where they bought into the lie that success equals happiness. After a lot of failing, they realized happiness comes instead from God-established rhythms in one's life.

Nick is a wannabe executive chef. Laura is a wannabe minimalist. Nick is an adventure-seeking, talkative extrovert. Laura is a homebody, book-hoarding introvert. Even as opposites, they unite in their lifelong goal to help people generate peace in their lives by stepping back, slowing down, and serving others.

Connect with *Love Fast Live Slow* by signing up as an insider at www.lovefastliveslow.com.

Visit
Lovefastliveslow.com

Check out our website today to continue the conversation about how to discover the simplicity of reflecting Jesus in a stressful world.

To find additional resources and share this *Love Fast Live Slow* journey with us, connect with us at:

www.lovefastliveslow.com

www.facebook.com/lovefastliveslow

@lovefastliveslow

Become an insider on our email list for a **free gift** in your inbox today!

Coming Soon!

A 6-Week Study Guide of *Love Fast Live Slow* for small group curriculum

We will dive deeper into why God created us and how to awaken peace within our souls. You will have everything you need to start applying these LFLS principles to your life

To stay in the loop, take the steps on this page
www.lovefastliveslow.com/takeaction

For additional bible study resources,
check out our recent 10-day devotionals on Amazon:

Hidden Heroes: How God Uses Everyday People to Change the World by Laura Mendenhall

Almost Heroes: How God's People Can Ruin a Good Thing by Laura Mendenhall

Made in the USA
Coppell, TX
26 June 2020